MANIFESTO
FOR A MORAL
REVOLUTION

MANIFESTO
FOR A MORAL
REVOLUTION

Practices to Build
a Better World

JACQUELINE NOVOGRATZ

HENRY HOLT AND COMPANY   New York

Henry Holt and Company
Publishers since 1866
120 Broadway
New York, New York 10271
www.henryholt.com

Henry Holt® and ® are registered trademarks of Macmillan Publishing
Group, LLC.

Lines from "The Pedagogy of Conflict" by Pádraig Ó Tuama, originally
published in *Sorry for Your Troubles* (Canterbury Press, 2013). Reprinted by
permission of author.

Library of Congress Cataloging-in-Publication Data

Names: Novogratz, Jacqueline, author.
Title: Manifesto for a moral revolution : practices to build
a better world / Jacqueline Novogratz.
Description: First edition. | New York : Henry Holt and Company, 2020.
Identifiers: LCCN 2019052281 (print) | LCCN 2019052282 (ebook) | ISBN
9781250222879 (hardcover) | ISBN 9781250759269 | ISBN 9781250222862
(ebook) | ISBN 9781250759269 (international edition)
Subjects: LCSH: Social responsibility of business. | Poverty.
Classification: LCC HD60 .N685 2020 (print) | LCC HD60 (ebook) | DDC
658.4/08—dc23
LC record available at https://lccn.loc.gov/2019052281
LC ebook record available at https://lccn.loc.gov/2019052282

Our books may be purchased in bulk for promotional, educational, or
business use. Please contact your local bookseller or the Macmillan
Corporate and Premium Sales Department at (800) 221-7945, extension
5442, or by e-mail at MacmillanSpecialMarkets@macmillan.com.

First Edition 2020

Designed by Meryl Sussman Levavi

Printed in the United States of America

1 2 3 4 5 6 7 8 9 10

To my parents,
Bob and Barbara Novogratz,
who taught me to love the world,
and
to all who aspire to give more
to the world than you take from it

CONTENTS

MANIFESTO
FOR A MORAL
REVOLUTION

INTRODUCTION

1986. Kigali, Rwanda. I am standing in a field on a blue-sky day, surrounded by tall, yellow sunflowers. I am a twenty-five-year-old former banker dressed in a flowy skirt, wearing flat, mud-speckled white shoes, my head filled with dreams of changing the world. Beside me is an apple-cheeked, bespectacled nun in a brown habit smiling broadly. Her name is Felicula, and I adore her for taking me under her wing. Along with a few other Rwandan women, she and I are planning to build the first microfinance bank in the country. Today, we're visiting a sunflower oil–pressing business, the kind of tiny venture our bank might one day support. We plan to call the microfinance organization Duterimbere, meaning "to go forward with enthusiasm."

All I see is upside.

* * *

2016. Kigali, Rwanda. I am standing at an outdoor reception on a starry night, surrounded by men and women in dark suits. I am the fifty-five-year-old CEO of Acumen, a global nonprofit seeking to change the way the world tackles poverty. Rwanda's president, Paul Kagame, and his top ministers are at the reception to meet potential investors in a new $70 million impact fund Acumen is building to bring solar electricity to more than ten million low-income people in East Africa.

I have become all too familiar with the risks of making and then trying to deliver on big promises. Yet I'm confident Acumen and its partners can launch and implement this fund, and thus prove the power of innovation to help solve one of the continent's most intractable problems.

Just before I begin to make a formal presentation to the group, a young Rwandan woman wearing a navy suit and low-heeled pumps approaches me.

"Ms. Novogratz," she says, "I think you knew my auntie."

"Really?" I ask. "What was her name?" I haven't a clue to whom she is referring: too many of my friends were murdered in the genocide.

"Her name was Felicula," she responds brightly.

My eyes well with tears. "I'm sorry," I stammer. "Would you remind me who you are again?"

"My name is Monique," the young woman answers with soft-spoken confidence, her eyes holding mine. "I am the deputy secretary-general of Rwanda's central bank."

Words fail me completely. I am transported back to the days when Felicula and I dreamed together of a world in which women would have greater control over their lives.

Of course, we started with a low bar: until 1986, it was illegal in Rwanda for a woman to open a bank account without her husband's permission. Although Felicula and I and our other cofounders had big dreams to make a difference, had you told us in 1986 that within a generation I would be standing before a young Rwandan woman charged with overseeing her nation's financial system, I'm not sure we would have believed you.

In addition to being an enterprising nun, Felicula Nyiramtarambirwa, along with two other cofounders of Duterimbere, was among the first three women parliamentarians in Rwandan history. Early in their parliamentary tenures, while Duterimbere was just getting started, the three women felt compelled to take on the issue of bride price, a system whereby men presented three cows to a potential father-in-law in exchange for marrying his daughter. Felicula especially respected the power of tradition, but not as an excuse for reducing women to chattel.

The bill to ban the payment of a bride price passed easily, but a backlash erupted. Rural women felt diminished. In their eyes, their economic value had been decimated overnight. Women and men across the country raised their voices in protest, and many parliamentarians blamed the outcry on the rashness of their freshmen colleagues. The women parliamentarians had failed to understand the depth of cultural practices in their own nation. They focused on what *could be*, but neglected to recognize the world that was, including the high-stakes realities of politics. In 1987, just a few days after the bride-price fiasco, Felicula was killed in a mysterious hit-and-run accident. Some assumed it was a government-orchestrated killing. The murderer was never found.

I mourned Felicula, and grieved over losing a person who gave me a sense of belonging without consideration of my tribe or religion or ethnicity. But if I had lost a chunk of my innocence with her death, I also had learned the folly and danger of unbridled optimism not grounded in the realities of the communities we wish to serve. I grew in understanding. And thanks to the elemental work contributed by Felicula and others, our microfinance bank expanded, reaching borrowers not only in Kigali but across the nation.

Then, in 1994, the Rwandan genocide ripped the country apart, resulting in the slaughter of more than a half million people, mostly from the minority Tutsi tribe. Shockingly, one of the cofounders of our beloved institution of social justice emerged as a leader of that horrendous bloodbath. After that, I couldn't help but question all those platitudes I'd heard about women being more nurturing and caring than men. *Some* women, I'd think. Not *all* women.

Yet, soon enough, like shoots of fragile flowers creeping upward through granite cracks, a small group of women leaders came together from across the country to put Duterimbere back together again. The quiet, resolute actions of these women who had lost everything but hope rekindled their resilience and helped repair the nation's broken heart.

Thirty years later, not only is Duterimbere surviving, but it is thriving, and continuing to play its part in Rwanda's remarkable recovery. And though the history of the country's first three women parliamentarians ended tragically, Rwanda now has the highest percentage of women parliamentarians of any country on earth.

Back in Kigali on that night in 2016, I reconnected with the memory of Felicula, who had started work she could not complete in her lifetime. She was taken too early, but her work continued anyway—because she cared, fought fiercely for her convictions, and brought others along with her. I was reminded that every one of us stands on the shoulders of those who have gone before, that every one of us has a chance to build on the collective knowledge of remarkable human beings, their achievements, the principles they cherished. And I was there to reassure myself that we have infinitely more knowledge, connection, tools, skills, and resources to tackle the world's injustices today than we did back in Felicula's time.

Or at any other time in history.

The poet T. S. Eliot wrote, "We shall not cease from exploration, and the end of all our exploring will be to arrive where we started and know the place for the first time." That night in Kigali, I renewed my commitment to working toward dreams so big that they may not be completed in *my* lifetime.

And I resolved to write a love letter of sorts to anyone daring to take action in our deeply flawed world.

We are made from what came before. We make *ourselves* out of the promises that lie ahead. And we are always in the process of becoming.

When I lived in Rwanda as a younger woman, cell phones, the internet, and social media had yet to be invented. I listened to the news twice daily via the BBC on a shortwave radio. It was a world of separation: separate nations, religions, ethnicities, tribes, and genders. Though that world was terribly unequal and unfair—nearly 40 percent of humanity subsisted on less than a dollar a day—most of us were blissfully unaware of what was happening in other parts of our own countries, let alone what was happening on other sides of the world.

The revolutions in technology and globalization in the past three decades have changed everything. The rate of extreme poverty has fallen to 10 percent and cell phones have connected nearly every individual on the planet. We can see into each other's living rooms and gain a view into one another's lifestyles. Rights for human beings—and nonhumans—are expanding. On so many dimensions, the world has gotten better.

Yet, the same forces that have shaped this world—technology and shareholder capitalism—hold within them the potential to destroy us. We are dangerously unequal and divided. We collectively face the ultimatum of our climate emergency. And many of the institutions devoted ostensibly to improving the lives of the many, not the few, are broken, yet we have not envisioned their replacements.

We need a new narrative. We are too entangled to abide worldviews based on separation, nor can we look to simple technological or market solutions. Those stories have run their course. We will be so much richer, productive, and peaceful if we learn not only to coexist but to flourish, celebrating our differences while holding to the understanding that we are part of each other, bound together by our shared humanity. That narrative will come not from above but from all of us.

What we need is a moral revolution, one that helps us reimagine and reform technology, business, and politics, thereby touching all aspects of our lives. By "moral," I don't mean strictly adhering to established rules of authority or convention regardless of consequence. I mean a set of principles focused on elevating our individual and collective dignity: a daily choice to serve others, not simply benefit ourselves. I mean complementing the audacity that built the world we know with a new humility more attuned to our interdependence.

Of course, the very notion of moral revolution is a tall order. Some might call it naïve. But I am not writing with wide-eyed idealism. Over three decades I have fought many fights for social and economic change. Much of this time has been spent building Acumen, investing in social entrepreneurs who seek to provide essential goods and services at affordable prices to people living in poverty. The work has given me a front-row seat to the realities of making sustainable change in some of the most challenging places on the planet. What I've learned from these individuals has deeply inspired me; and I want to pass on those lessons, because they apply broadly.

None of this is easy, of course. I have accompanied hundreds of change agents through challenges and sometimes crushing defeats. My face wears the lines of failures, losses, and far too many sleepless nights.

However, hard battles do not account for all my face's creases. Some are etched from smiles and laughter shared with people who insisted on striving for freedom, opportunity, and justice against all odds. I have partnered with good people who have changed their communities, their companies, their nations, and ultimately, themselves. I have witnessed people making what others might consider hopelessly romantic dreams come true—and true not just for a few, but for millions (in some cases, hundreds of millions). The actions of these people, not their slogans or pretty words, have kept alive for me the ideas of purpose, of impact, of dignity, of love—all separate points on a moral compass.

A new generation is rising, one that is more conscious of how they live, what they buy, and where they work. Many are unwilling to work for companies unless those companies are committed to sustainability and recognize that with power must come accountability. And a growing number of companies are listening. I've been heartened to see some CEOs move to stakeholder models, partly in response to prompting by their younger employees, and because they themselves recognize the need to change. If you are working in a corporation, you have ample opportunity to act.

Cynics might point to a system of governments, corporations, and technologies so broken that attempts to change it from the edges are futile. But cynics don't build the future. Instead, they often use their jaundiced views to justify inaction.

And never before have we more desperately needed their opposite—thoughtful, empathetic, resilient believers and optimists on a path of moral leadership.

This book assumes that you are interested in being part of world-changing human capital that will help solve problems big and small. Maybe you are a teacher or a communicator, an activist or a doctor, a lawyer or an investor, or some new force for positive change. I have seen people like you alter the lives of schoolchildren and street children, refugees, the formerly incarcerated; of people living in forgotten communities and in places ravaged by war, poverty, or toxic industries. I've witnessed you not just doing but improving the often-unseen work of serving the sick, healing the heartbroken, sitting with the dying to remind others that they, too, are good and worthy of love.

Or you might be a philanthropist. The hard work of changing systems requires financial resources. And just as there is a new generation of entrepreneurial individuals focused on solving complex issues, so there is a new generation of philanthropists, men and women willing to give not just money but time, commitment, connections, and big parts of their hearts and minds.

Change is the domain of all of us.

In every country on earth, people are refusing to acquiesce to the exhausting, deadening news cycles filled with catastrophe and cynicism, seeking to make good news instead. These people are deliberately expanding their circles of compassion, reaching across lines of difference with a quiet strength forged in all that we have in common. Our problems are so similar, so solvable. And we are better than we think we are.

Those I've known who've most changed the world exhibit a voracious curiosity about the world and other people, and a willingness to listen and empathize with those unlike them. These people stand apart not because of school degrees or the size of their bank accounts, but because of their character, their willingness to build reservoirs of courage and stand for their beliefs, even if they stand alone.

Of course, this kind of character isn't built overnight. It is honed through a lifelong process of committing to something bigger than yourself, aspiring to qualities of moral leadership, defining success by how others fare because of your efforts, embedding a sense of purpose into your daily decisions.

Change is possible. And *because* large-scale, sustainable change is possible, I have come to see it as a responsibility to be part of that change.

When it comes to a life of making change, there are no shortcuts. It is hard work, but it is time well spent. And when you reach the other side of the difficult-to-see tangible transformation, it is like nothing in the world: a deep, abiding sense not just of accomplishment but of joy.

I wrote this book because I believe that our fragile, unequal, divided, yet still beautiful, world deserves a radical moral rejuvenation. This revolution will ask all of us to shift our ways of thinking to connection rather than consumerism, to purpose rather than profits, to sustainability rather than selfishness. We must awaken to see workers not as inputs, the environment not as our personal domain, and shareholders not as all-powerful. And we need to move away from old models of doing what is right for me and assuming it will turn out right for you.

If you are looking for a simple how-to guide or step-by-step instructions for building a company or a nonprofit organization, this is not the book for you. Rather, this book is my attempt to bring forward and share the principles I've learned from thousands of change agents, based above all on the value of human dignity. Each of their stories makes manifest the kind of moral leadership that looks to the future not with blind optimism but with a hard-edged hope. The people whose work I describe in this book have had to learn to deal with ugly truths while singing songs of the possible. They recognize that every problem is an opportunity for us to act.

A manifesto is a public declaration of intentions. This one is for all who hear the call of moral leadership—guiding principles to dream and build a better world, coordinates of a moral compass set by those already leading this journey of change.

Hopefully, this is for you.

Chapter 1

JUST START

A few years ago, I spoke at a small women's university in the American South. After my talk, I had the privilege of sitting with a number of the school's top students. For several hours, we talked about what was wrong in the world and what each of us might do about it. "What do *you* dream of doing?" I finally asked a bespectacled blond woman who had been listening intently without uttering a word.

"I want to change the world."

"How might you do that?" I asked.

"That's the problem," she said. "I have no idea."

Tears welled in her eyes. For a moment, I caught a glimpse of my younger self.

I remembered looking out at a world I wanted to change and having no clue as to how to do it. I was at once wildly bold and quietly frightened, feeling that a bull and a dove coexisted inside me, worried that I lacked the skills or the know-how to pull off my ambitions. And some of those feelings continued even when I became more certain of possible paths forward.

In fact, many of the words and questions from the students

that night sounded familiar. How can I be of use? How can I find my purpose? Where will I make the most impact?

When we look back on our lives, we construct sense-making narratives of who we are and how we've chosen to spend our time. But when we look forward, the path ahead can feel overwhelmingly elusive. While the fearful student and her friends pushed for answers, I could offer only questions and a single piece of advice. For while there are skills to gain and character traits to develop, there is only one way to begin.

Just start—and let the work teach you.

Too many who yearn to make a difference become paralyzed by the fear of leaping without having worked out every detail. Yet the decision we face is not to chart the perfect way forward; it is simply to embark on a journey. Once we've taken a step forward, the work will teach us where to take a second step, and then a third, and so on. Purpose does not reveal itself to those sitting safely at the starting block. In other words, you don't *plan* your way into finding your purpose. You live into it.

Childhood memories and reveries, however distant, can provide clues to our innermost yearnings. As a little girl, I read stories of the saints. They were printed on cards that my beloved first-grade teacher, Sister Mary Theophane, gave me for doing well on tests. Many decades later, my friend the poet Marie Howe suggested that the stories of the saints marked the first time we little Catholic girls read of women who wrote the narratives of their own lives. The saints were also the first people I encountered who lived for, and were often willing to die for, an idea bigger than themselves. Their resolution and valor infected me with a desire to be of use; I wanted to be like them somehow.

When I was ten, my fifth-grade teacher, Mrs. Howerton, introduced me to a row of biographies of heroic figures, little yellow books hidden in a corner of the school library. There I'd sit cross-legged on the floor and disappear into the worlds of the abolitionist Harriet Tubman, the pioneering doctor Elizabeth Blackwell, the human rights advocate Eleanor Roosevelt, and so on. These women refused to be limited by small dreams, and though I was not yet able to point to a living example of a woman like them, they stood as beacons of the possible, of lives lived to make a difference.

But if I dreamed of becoming a warrior for love and justice, my first job out of university hardly fit the bill. For more than three years, I spent my days on Wall Street as an analyst at Chase Manhattan Bank. Though I hadn't planned on becoming a banker, I discovered a delight in building financial skills and in understanding the workings of economic systems, not to mention the side benefit of traveling the world. Until then, I had never left the United States. That banking job took me to forty countries, and exposed me to political and economic realities that I'd previously only studied in books.

What I didn't like about banking, though, was the way our financial system excluded low-income people from borrowing funds that could change their lives and contribute to their local economies. Banks required borrowers to put up twice the value of their loans as collateral, a requirement out of reach for even the lower-middle class. The private sector was set up to earn profits, not to ensure that multiple stakeholders, especially the poor, were well served. Understanding they had little chance of being part of the mainstream financial system, most low-income people dared not even walk through the doors of the major banks.

As the months at Chase passed, a yearning to do something for lower-income people took root inside me. That yearning was a clue to the thread I should follow, a stirring driven by a growing sense of injustice and a desire to contribute. A weekend in mid-1985 spent walking in the favelas of Rio de Janeiro, conversing with hardworking people about their aspirations and realities, convinced me of what I already knew to be true: nations would develop equitably only if their low-income citizens could save and borrow.

Around that time, a friend showed me an article about a little-known economist named Muhammad Yunus who had started a tiny operation in Bangladesh called the Grameen Bank. Grameen was part of a fledgling sector called microfinance, which included the Self-Employed Women's Association, in India; the Bangladesh Rural Advancement Committee (BRAC); and Women's World Banking, in the United States. These institutions made small loans (from thirty to one hundred dollars, on average) to millions of low-income people, mostly women, so that they could build tiny businesses to support their lives.

Though only about ten years old at the time, the microfinance sector already was yielding noteworthy results. Grameen Bank had accumulated data showing that poor women repaid their loans at much higher rates than their wealthy counterparts. That got my attention. I started to dream of leaving Wall Street to work in microfinance.

However, I first had to overcome my fear of diminished personal income and an even stronger fear of my parents' disappointment. I was raised the eldest of seven in a military family and had had to pay my way through university and take on debt to graduate. Chase had set me squarely on the path to wealth and a vision of a future with the bank was tempting. Also, a senior officer at Chase had recently offered me a fast-track position that would give me the chance to break barriers for women in the financial world.

My father did not want me to pass up what he saw as a once-in-a-lifetime career opportunity. My mother worried that something bad might happen to me if I worked in a developing country—or worse, I might never get married. And, of course, neither of them wanted me to move to another continent; parents want to keep their children safe. It did not help that my friends worried that our relationships would change, and some simply thought I'd lost my mind.

The small voice inside me was shouted down by the cacophony. I was a born pleaser and cared about what others thought. But this tendency naturally butted heads with another side of me, which was daring, justice-seeking, sometimes even reckless, determined to make a difference in the world.

Somehow I knew that if I didn't dare then, I might never take the risk. Though only twenty-five years old, I could already name peers who lived provisionally, promising they'd follow their dreams *after* they paid off their debts . . . or married . . . or got an MBA. Over time, their lives had become more expensive to manage, making it even harder for them to take the leap. I feared living a life of quiet desperation, to quote Thoreau, and was hungry for a life rich in adventure.

Some people felt wholly alive in the world of finance; that wasn't me. I needed to venture toward a different life. Yes, I had significant student debt to repay, but I would figure out the dollars and cents of it all later.

After a few months of research, I discovered what sounded like an amazing opportunity: to work with numerous fledgling microfinance organizations across a whole continent, providing management support and serving as an ambassador to women interested in using small business as a tool for change. However, there was a hitch: the job was based in Côte d'Ivoire, West Africa, not in Brazil, where I'd hoped to work. If I was going to make a sacrifice of career and income, I reasoned, I should sacrifice for a place whose intoxicating rhythms and colors held special appeal to me. I knew almost nothing about the Côte d'Ivoire.

Alas, no opportunity in Brazil was on the table, and I had to make a choice. I could focus on the substance of my desire, to become a bridge between low-income people and the world of finance, or I could obsess over my fantasy of living in Brazil. I couldn't do both.

The Jesuits have a powerful saying: "Go where your deepest yearning meets the world's greatest need." I yearned to contribute to the economic development of low-income people, to learn about the world, to live in a new culture. For whatever reason, the world seemed to need, or at least *want*, me more in West Africa than in Brazil.

So, I took the job in West Africa. I just started.

I don't mean to sound cavalier when I say "just start." I was lucky to grow up with parents who ultimately supported my decisions. That is not the case for many who face heavy implications for rejecting the wishes of their families, clans, and religious leaders. Indeed, for some people, just starting a *conversation* can take gumption. Moreover, there was truth in my parents' fears: bad things *did* happen to me, and it *did* take much longer for me to tie the knot than they (or I) would have imagined.

But no one escapes life without being wounded and scarred; and I had multiple chances to wed, including when I lived in Africa. Over the years, I came to see that there are many ways to live a life. I was "enough" on my own terms. It would take until I was forty to meet my husband, Chris, and only then did I realize that I'd been waiting for the love of my life.

Young people sometimes ask, "But what if I dare and then fail?" I failed more times than I can count. I moved to Côte d'Ivoire and was met with outright rejection from those I had hoped to serve. Yet I learned from my failures, and came to understand that to rule out failure is to rule out success.

With each experience, the good, the bad, and even the ugly, I added tools to my toolbox. More important, I honed my understanding of myself and how others perceived me, preparing to listen, learn, and work in partnership. I began to comprehend that the world does not need another hero—sustained change results from multiple heroic acts across a community—and that it was my job to help others shine.

Of course, there are times when nothing seems to be working, when you don't understand what is going on around you, and no one trusts you enough to tell you. But what separates those who dabble in feel-good endeavors and those who actually nudge the world forward has nothing to do with intellect, connections, or specific skills. The ones whose actions and ideas produce positive consequences are the ones who stay in the game.

Try. Fail. Then try again. Follow the thread as it unspools. Just start.

* * *

After my bumpy start in Côte d'Ivoire, I moved to Kenya for a few months, where I continued to stumble in my efforts to "do good." Finally, in early 1987, when I was still twenty-five, I accepted a three-week consultancy in Kigali, Rwanda, to research the state of credit for low-income women. It became clear that the only way to change the financial standing of the women there was to build an institution tailored to their needs. I didn't slow down to ask myself who was I to try to create a financial institution based on a measly three years' credit experience as a baby banker at Chase. I saw a problem to be solved—the banking system excluded people who were just asking for a fair chance to borrow and contribute to the economy. And I was already meeting extraordinary local women who would partner with me.

Who was I *not* to dare?

Duterimbere, Rwanda's first microfinance bank, which I cofounded with Felicula and others, carved a lending path for the country's low-income women and touched the lives of many thousands. It also changed my life, for good. Experiencing firsthand the power of markets from the perspectives of low-income women reinforced my belief in using the tools of capitalism to enable individual freedom.

The work gave me new insights and skills. In 1987, I witnessed how global market fluctuations caused local coffee prices to plunge, devastating the livelihoods of 80 percent of Rwandan farmers—an episode that woke me to the perils of unbridled capitalism. Had I not taken that first leap from Wall Street, I would not have learned this. And had I not persevered after failing in Côte d'Ivoire, I might have gone home without confronting my own limitations or discovering my truest gifts. We grow when we stretch, when we are willing to embrace the uncomfortable.

***

"Just start" is a mind-set that belongs not only to the young, but to anyone who hopes to remain productive, vibrant, and relevant throughout their lives. No one taught me about the elixir of self-renewal like my mentor, the venerable public servant John Gardner. I met John during my first year of business school, just after my initial stretch of work in Africa, and he represented precisely the kind of leader I aspired to become. Though I didn't fully understand it at the time, I've discovered that when you don't know where to start, following a leader who inspires you can be a powerful strategy.

John started and restarted throughout his life, participating in his generation's most momentous decisions, yet remaining free from society's pressures to be what others thought he should be. The sole Republican in President Lyndon Johnson's cabinet, John served as secretary of health, education, and welfare during America's civil rights movement, during which he started the White House Fellows program and launched Medicare, among other initiatives. In 1968, he resigned his prestigious position in protest of the Vietnam War and had to start again.

Two years later, at age fifty-four, John founded Common Cause, a grassroots citizens' movement to hold government accountable. And in 1980, he cofounded Independent Sector to support the nonprofit sector. Though in his seventies when I met him, John would go on to cofound a nonprofit organization, now called Encore, that inspires older people to just start again themselves by getting involved in service organizations across the country.

John's was a lived and practical wisdom. "The self-renewing man," he wrote, "looks forward to an endless and unpredictable dialogue between his potentialities and the claims of life—not only the claims he encounters but the claims he invents." He was a half century older than me, but John's enduring curiosity, his sense of possibility and willingness to try made him seem the youngest person I knew.

So, just start. Find mentors you can learn from, whether in person, online, or in print. And let your experiences teach you what you have to do next. All in all, it took me nearly twenty years of apprenticing, putting new tools in my toolbox, and expanding my understanding of the world through jobs in banking, development, and foundations, before my skills, aspirations, and networks came together to create Acumen in 2001.

I was ready to just start again. I had a theory of how we might revolutionize philanthropy by investing it as long-term, patient capital in intrepid entrepreneurs daring to build financially sustainable solutions to poverty where markets and governments had both failed the poor. But I didn't have many proof points. I remember privately thinking that I would spend three years doing all I could to build a "blueprint for change," and then decide whether Acumen was an idea worth trying beyond that.

Luckily, I was part of a group of pioneering individuals who were willing to risk their philanthropy and give their time for an idea most considered crazy.

That early group cheered on every move forward. At each step, the work, and sometimes the world, taught us what we had to do. When the 9/11 terror attacks changed the global landscape, my team and I decided to work in the Muslim world. That same thread of human dignity that had pulled me into microfinance drew my team to invest in Pakistan, a place previously unknown to me. After ten years of work in South Asia and Africa, we wanted to do more to attack the poverty of inequality, and so we expanded to Latin America and the United States. Each new geography was a risk, each an adventure.

Each new investment deepened our understanding of how the world works—and gave us confidence to push the edges of our work even further. When our companies identified the need for talent, not just money, we launched a Fellows program to support entrepreneurial leaders. When more people applied to become fellows than we could directly support, we developed an online school for social change. When we found ourselves unsatisfied with conventional impact measurements, we created our own approach to measuring what matters. One thing led to another, each new step made possible because we had started in the first place.

Nearly twenty years have passed with Acumen. When we started, I couldn't have dreamed the kinds of companies we would help build: rule-breaking, yet highly successful enterprises unleashing the potential of millions of low-income people. I wouldn't have understood the kinds of partnerships needed to bring critical services not to just some people but to all. And though we made a few false starts, to be sure, because of our efforts and those of so many others around the world, a new sector exists, called impact investing. And a new generation has a newer, better set of tools with which to reimagine and build models of inclusive and environmentally sustainable capitalism.

All these years later, I am still just starting. I am honing my purpose, clarifying who I am and want to become.

And I have found in the idea of human dignity a purpose for which I am willing to live—and, if necessary, to die. And that has made all the difference.

You may not yet have a crystal-clear sense of *your* purpose. That's okay. It will grow with you. But if you have an inkling that you'd like your life to be about something bigger than yourself, listen to that urge. Follow the thread. The world needs you.

Just start.

Chapter 2

REDEFINE SUCCESS

On the morning of India's winter solstice in December 2015, Ankit Agarwal could not have imagined that a bunch of floating flowers would change his life's trajectory. Ankit was showing Jakub, a friend visiting from the Czech Republic, the sights of his hometown, Kanpur, an industrial city known for its textile and leather tanning factories, built on the banks of the great Ganges, one of Hinduism's most sacred rivers. The two young men sat on the steps leading down to the Ganges, musing on the meaning of life. As the two conversed, thousands of the faithful and tradition-bound entered the waters to mark the shortest day of the year with blessings and ablutions—and flowers. It was a scene Ankit had witnessed throughout his life, a colorful but blurry backdrop to his days.

Despite recent success in his early career, Ankit was full of angst. He was pondering aloud what it would take to find contentment and success when Jakub interrupted him, pointing to the river as if he'd not heard a word from his friend. Little did Jakub know that his distraction would be the key to

Ankit's destiny. "Why is India's most sacred river so polluted with an endless float of dead flowers?" Jakub asked.

Ankit had always taken for granted the sight of marigolds, roses, jasmine, and other blossoms drifting in the Ganges. Daily, millions of people across India brought flowers and foodstuffs to Hindu temples as blessings for the gods. Unwilling to desecrate these blessings by disposing of them in the trash, priests dumped them in sacred rivers. Rotting flowers and foodstuffs in the water was just the way things were.

"But look at the scum of chemicals floating on the water's surface," Jakub rejoined, surveying the clothed men and women wading in the river. "And imagine what those pesticides and chemicals emanating from the flowers are doing to those believers as they wade in carcinogenic water."

At first, Ankit shrugged off his friend's observation. He knew the Ganges was highly polluted; he had even visited some of the factories along the river's banks. But the sight of those riotous rotting flowers got under his skin. How, he wondered, could a tradition considered so essential and so gentle have such ugly ramifications? And how bad could it be?

That moment awakened Ankit's curiosity and offered him a thread to follow, one that drove his sense of possibility and unleashed his powers of innovation. The deeper he dove into the question of solving the "flower issue," the more he began to open himself to a more profound meaning of success. And for him, the timing was right.

Four and a half years earlier, Ankit had reported to his first job after university as a newly minted engineer. Waiting in the company's reception area, he had noticed a wall filled with portraits of every employee who'd won patents. "I want this. I want my picture there," he told himself. Success, or at least happiness, began to look like a portrait with a metal plate inscribed with his name.

So, Ankit drove himself relentlessly, staying late to complete tasks, often sleeping in the office. Just three years later, he became one of the youngest engineers in the company's history with a plaque on that wall. The whole team applauded.

Then a strange thing happened. "Instead of jumping with happiness, it was as if suddenly everything seemed meaningless," Ankit explained to me in an email. "I started to ask what I wanted to do in life, and began to feel the whole rush was meaningless."

There had to be more to life than prizes, awards, titles, or salaries. At age twenty-five, Ankit understood that his success would come only from focusing on a "challenge that would improve lives or the earth, really, *anything* that would bring about real change."

Those flowers floating in the river transformed into blessings for Ankit. Here was a chance to solve a problem that mattered. Changing the ancient practice of dumping flowers into the rivers would require confronting a status quo solidified over many generations. Ankit knew he would go from being viewed as successful to being considered crazy by some. But he had attempted the conventional route to success and found it less than fulfilling. Now he had a chance to redefine success for himself. Crazy might be just the ticket.

In researching the "temple flower problem," Ankit discovered that Indians discarded more than eight million tons of flowers yearly into rivers such as the Ganges. The flowers are covered in a variety of pesticides, including arsenic, lead, and cadmium, all of which contribute to water-borne diseases. The more complex the problem revealed itself to be, the less Ankit connected success to himself and instead focused on changing the entire system.

He partnered with his best friend, Karan Rastogi, to create Phool, a company that would solve multiple problems at once. Phool, in Hindi, means flower. Success to the company meant the improved health of the Ganges, measured by the number of tons of flowers the company was able to retrieve from the temples. Success would also be measured by the number of jobs the company created, and particularly by the quality of jobs for disadvantaged people.

To realize these elements of success required a for-profit model, according to the two entrepreneurs, one that ensured financial sustainability and attracted enough capital to meet the scale of the problem they were trying to solve. Profits were an important indicator, but the true measure of their venture's success would be its impact on all stakeholders, including employees and the earth.

And, of course, customers. To this end, Ankit and Karan needed a salable product. They reasoned that a growing group of consumers was interested in products built on principles of the circular economy, systems that removed "waste" from the production cycle by finding ways to reuse and repurpose it. Ankit and Karan asked themselves what they could produce from the flower waste that people would want to buy, and how that product would improve people's lives. They spent eighteen months listening to potential customers and trying to understand what they might value.

One ingenious product they settled on was incense sticks. Used for cultural and religious practice, incense is burned daily in many Indian households; however, the majority of sticks are made from charcoal, which negatively affects respiratory health. Ankit and Karan reasoned that they could use what was already being treated as waste to make flower incense sticks that were healthier and of lower cost. The flower incense sticks would require minimal skills to produce and would embody the spirit of the temples from which the flowers came.

Phool now collects about ten thousand pounds of flowers daily from Kanpur's temples. The company provides each temple with large bins, which are routinely picked up and taken to a plant, essentially a warehouse and drying area. To eliminate the flower waste's toxicity, the company sprays it with an organic Bioculum. Scores of women then separate the petals to transform dried organic waste into incense sticks and warming compost.

As part of their commitment to sustainable business practices, Phool's founders dedicated themselves to hiring women from the manual scavenger caste, one of the most marginalized groups on earth. Though the caste system is technically outlawed in India, more than three-quarters of a million "scavengers" are still consigned to removing untreated human waste (using flimsy tools such as cardboard, tin plates, and buckets) from toilets and pit latrines, which they then must sometimes carry several kilometers before reaching a disposal site.

These "scavengers" suffer extreme prejudice, often living at the margins and carrying a heavy yoke of poverty. Especially in the company's early years, the Phool founders' commitment to hiring women from this caste added complexity and cost to building their business. The scavenger community was located at the edges of town, so the company sought to hire a bus to transport the women to and from work. But it took two months to convince a bus company to drive them. Then, when the owner of Phool's first rented space got wise to the employees' caste, he destroyed the factory's equipment and summarily threw the company out.

Though Phool sustained devastating financial losses, Ankit and Karan started over, persisting through clenched teeth. Ankit's dream of success had evolved from the days when only traditional honors mattered to him, and the founders weren't going to be cowed by other people's narrow-mindedness. As the level of difficulty rose, so did their commitment to realizing their dream.

In January 2018, Acumen's India director Mahesh Yagnaraman and I visited Ankit, an Acumen fellow, at his factory. Wearing a black leather jacket and jeans, he greeted us in the open-air courtyard of his factory, where rows of women sat on tiny plastic stools, concentrating as they sifted through tangerine, bright yellow, and white flowers. Inside the warehouse, other women stood in long lines rolling incense sticks with speed and precision. I tried my hand at rolling the sticks, and gained instant respect for the women who worked at Phool. Meanwhile, the women couldn't stop laughing at the mess I made.

Our little Acumen group sat for a while in a small room that abutted the courtyard with Ankit and his wife, Ridhima, discussing Phool's business fundamentals. Ankit spoke with both toughness and tenderness, making it clear that Phool's mission to clean the rivers and provide dignified jobs drove every decision the company made. Only *then* do they make the numbers work, understanding that it may take a long time to build a profitable business that stays true to all its goals.

The company is committed to its employees first. In addition to providing daily transport, Phool pays well, provides health insurance, and serves the women tea twice daily. It also encourages the women to take a bottle of clean water home to their families at the end of each day. I asked Ankit why he sent the water home with them.

"Society reminds these women nearly every moment of their lives that they are outcastes. They are unwanted. But when you can drink the same water as others do, finally you can feel equal," he responded.

We soon moved to the courtyard outside the warehouse, where a vibrant, multicolored carpet of flowers had been laid out for drying. A group of women sitting by the flowers had taken a break for lunch. I requested to join them and asked how their lives had changed since working with Ankit and Karan. "I love coming here," said a freckled woman with smiling eyes, her hair pulled back. "Before this company, I had to move from house to house for work and never feel respected. Life was very difficult. Here, we learn new skills. We're with friends."

Another jumped in: "This is the first time anyone has tried to teach us something. Sometimes I worry that I'm not learning fast enough. But these people believe I can do it, and that gives me confidence. I'm bolder now at home and in my community. I'm able to keep up with school fees for the first time, too."

Another woman added, "I bought my family our first television, and now the neighbors come over to my house to watch."

A fourth chimed in, stating, "They respect us in this place. We don't have to sit on the ground." I told her I didn't understand. "This seat," she said, pointing to the two-dollar plastic stool beneath her, "is the first one anyone has ever offered to me."

As our discussion continued, the women avoided any talk of caste, understandably distancing themselves from all-too-recent humiliations and heartbreaks engendered from belonging to a group deemed "untouchable." They euphemistically referred to their past jobs cleaning up waste as "domestic work," and quickly steered the conversation to their present states of happiness. I was touched by the women's gratitude for the opportunity of decent work that entailed neither degradation nor abuse.

A woman in a caramel sweater over a yellow kurta, quiet till then, added her voice to the conversation. "It is so good here," she said. "We feel fresh being around the flowers. I like the smell. And it is good that our work brings blessings back to the gods."

She was referring to the virtuous cycle of these flowers, collected from temples and converted into incense sticks before being returned to the temples as a second round of offerings. The woman did not mention that many households that purchased the sticks would nonetheless refuse to allow the women who produced them to enter their homes.

"Is there anything you would change at the company?" I asked.

The woman with smiling eyes responded, "I only want this place to succeed. We must work hard here to help it grow. That's all. I only worry that one day it might move from here."

By then, Ankit had walked up, himself a paradox of presentation and values. His somber mien belied the tenderness with which he spoke to the women. "We're not going anywhere," he assured them gently.

To some, Ankit and Karan's choice of whom to hire and how to manage those employees seemed noble but, ultimately, misguided. It is challenging to make any company profitable, and they could have taken a much easier path to building a business. But Ankit and Karan define success in terms that include more than money.

Imagine the women gossiping and laughing as they travel in the bus driven specifically for them. Consider what it might feel like to have tea served to you when you've been considered less worthy than other people your entire life. Or the joy that comes from earning enough money to experience a level of self-reliance you've never before had. Picture their children, who now receive fresh drinking water each night, some of them for the first time. Laughter, respect, the security of productive work, a sense of belonging, *dignity*—these are things that matter the most to our experience as human beings, yet our financial and economic systems too often fail to acknowledge them when calculating "success."

Although it may take time to change ancient practices, Phool is using modern market incentives grounded in moral values. This combination of fundamentals bodes well not only for the company's long-term financial sustainability but for a sense of shared success. The temple priests feel proud that they no longer are polluting rivers in the name of the gods. The men who collect the flowers have good, decent jobs. The rivers are cleaner, making the pilgrims who bathe in the Ganges and other rivers less likely to fall sick. And consumers know that by purchasing these high-quality goods, which have been produced sustainably, they are providing jobs and dignity to some of the most disadvantaged women in India. That is the kind of success everyone can feel good partaking in.

Success doesn't just wait for us on a distant horizon. Success is within all of us, waiting for us to live into it. It exists in the beauty we create, the goodwill we offer, the ideas we spread, the causes for which we stand, and the lives we help transform. It shows up in the health and well-being of our children, our communities; in the way we love the world and one another. Even if this particular venture fails, Ankit is already a very successful man, allowing curiosity and a desire to serve others to guide his life choices.

Of course, the notion of redefining success rubs against the status quo. Humans are status-seeking beings. We yearn to be accepted, respected, loved. Our current systems (economic, political, and social) reinforce a definition of "winning" based on money, power, and fame. Rather than being rewarded for what we give, we're too often affirmed by what we take.

What if our Golden Rule were not only "Do unto others as you would have them do unto you" but also "Give more to the world than you take from it"? That would change everything. If enough of us pursued that path, the world of inequality, exploitation, and injustice would slowly be replaced by a world of inclusion, fairness, and dignity.

The point is this: *We* are the system. We decide how to define success, and we can reject purely individualistic terms. There is much to learn from cultural approaches that value sustainability over economic progress, or that build in practices to keep the community more equal. Shiroi Lily Shaiza, an Acumen fellow from Nagaland, a state in Northeast India, shared with me how her ancestors practiced "the feast of merit."

"When a community member earned significant wealth, he would be required to host enormous feasts for the community," she said. "The person would consider it the highest honor. He would be entitled to wear a special cloak and ornament his house to signify his high social standing. And the villagers revered that person as the pinnacle of success, especially those wealthy people who, by the end of their lives, had given everything away."

Every generation has the opportunity to renew the values, systems, and structures that define their societies, and to jettison those that no longer serve. The most enduring systems are those grounded in fundamental values based on human flourishing. We can disagree on the specifics of what humans need to succeed, but if our starting point is an environmentally sustainable world that enables all its inhabitants to flourish, then we've got the foundation for a moral framework. Unequal systems persist, yet they can be reimagined and reformed when people muster enough awareness and collective determination to do something about them.

It goes without saying that systems do not change overnight. In the meantime, the world needs brave people to create models of companies, organizations, schools, religious institutions, hospitals, prisons, and governments designed for a world interdependent and environmentally at risk. The best will drive themselves relentlessly, exposing their hearts to the world, understanding that others' resistance to change is part of the deal we make when we sign up to reject the status quo. Setbacks are inevitable, yet as most anyone who has ever tried to change anything will tell you, it is the difficult, not the easy, that underlies those accomplishments that ultimately imbue our souls with the kind of success that sustains.

* * *

Sometimes, when we are pursuing intrinsically-driven accomplishments, progress can feel so unbearably slow that even those who have already redefined success for themselves must reevaluate before renewing their commitment to the work they know is right for them. Benje Williams spent 2011 in Lahore, Pakistan, as an Acumen fellow building an outreach team for a drinking water company that served local slum areas. Less than 5 percent of Pakistani youths are educated beyond high school, and as Benje explained, "I was unprepared for the difficulty of hiring a workforce trained not just in technical skills but in critical life skills."

Benje began to dream about building a leadership and

workforce development institute that would train millions of young unemployed and underemployed Pakistanis—part of the "youth bulge" defining Pakistan and most of the developing world. (Sixty-four percent of Pakistan's population is under age thirty, the highest percentage of young people in the world.)

"Pakistan's youthful generation is a national asset," Benje explained during one of my visits, "but only if young people are able to obtain the necessary skills to widen their opportunities. Otherwise, an untrained, excluded, and frustrated youth population will pose a serious problem for the country and beyond."

A few years subsequent to his Acumen Fellowship experience and after earning a degree from Stanford Graduate School of Business, Benje returned to Lahore and founded Amal Academy, a nonprofit leadership organization to train first-generation graduates from secondary- and tertiary-level universities and place them in good jobs.

This work challenged Benje on every front. He was a foreigner with no financial resources of his own, there was no institution of its kind in the country, and those he served had little or no income to spend. Nonetheless, Benje created several partnerships that provided revenue and trained hundreds of young people in the organization's first few years. His reputation for effectiveness was spreading, and his commitment to his work made him beloved in the local community. Yet, to Benje, something was amiss.

Despite meaningful progress, there are times in every change-maker's journey when questions and doubts grow, multiplying like weeds until you feel you might suffocate. In January 2016, three years after he founded Amal Academy, Benje asked if he could come see me when he was passing through New York. I invited him to join me for a 6 a.m. run along the Hudson River. The bitter cold, windy morning was matched by a heaviness in Benje's usually sunny demeanor.

"What's up?" I asked.

"I'm not sure we're doing enough," he said.

The statement stopped me in my tracks.

"I started Amal to change the education system, not simply to help a few young people," Benje explained.

I reminded him that "hundreds" did not constitute a few. From my perspective, he was right on track, three years in, building a business model that could significantly impact lives and cover its costs. I'd always found Benje exceptional in every way—relentless in focus, uncomplaining, effective, always putting others before himself. I wondered what was eating at his soul.

Then I remembered: when Benje studied at Stanford, he was confronted by the lure of conventional success as defined by outsized salaries and enviable job titles. Some students there convinced themselves that they had competed in a "meritocracy" and "earned" whatever they got. But Benje lived with a different ethos. He understood that the lottery of life puts humans in a great variety of starting positions and that luck often trumps merit. Benje yearned to be of use. To make the right career choice, he'd had to limit his options.

"The only way I knew to stay true to myself," he once told me, "was to wear blinders during the job recruitment season, and not apply for a single job. I didn't want to be tempted by a position with a huge salary. I even deactivated Facebook and Instagram because the comparison game can be so paralyzing."

Many of us will repeatedly face the choice of whether to make money or make a difference. And though you *can* have both, there nonetheless will be times when you must decide which value is of greater priority. Benje had gone all in to serve the disadvantaged and make a positive difference. Given how long it can take to create a significant, sustained impact, for people with grand ambition, that decision undoubtedly leads to moments of great stress.

"You're doing what you set out to do," I reminded him. "Be proud of what you've built. Most people talk about change. You're *doing* it. And you've only started."

I hated seeing Benje be so hard on himself. I also could recognize my younger self in him. I, too, had gone all in for a life of social impact, and I knew well the feeling that the marketing genius Seth Godin "calls "the Dip," that moment (which can feel like forever) when the thing you think you want to do has gotten so hard that you don't know if it will ever work or become enjoyable.

Problems seem much easier to solve from a distance. New jobs seem easier to obtain; new organizations, easier to navigate. But that is not how most turn out to be. When confronting on-ground realities, our expectations regarding not only results, but also rewards, both psychological and financial, diminish.

There have been periods in my life when the work felt so hard for so long that the Dip threatened to take up permanent residence inside me. Those were not times of crisis—for emergencies focus my energies. In those times, like many entrepreneurs, I can muster the power to break through walls. Instead, the Dip would present itself during the doldrums like a weighty tumor growing thicker and heavier, making even fairly minor tasks feel Sisyphean.

My blues hurt more because everyone around me appeared to be doing fabulously. During my thirties in particular—I was around the same age as Benje at the time of our morning jog—I saw many friends from business school go to work at technology start-ups likely to make them wealthy or marry people who were themselves financial success stories. If they didn't have a powerful career, they had a beautiful house filled with perfectly behaved, well-dressed children. Single, without kids, financially stressed, and unable to describe my work in ways most could understand, I spent more than a few lonely nights asking myself if I was enough.

Three years into something new is often just the moment you hit the Dip: the excitement of your ambition to change the world somehow fades into the reality of daily frustrations and creeping fears. Staff members don't show up. Funders tell you they'd like to see more proof of your concept, yet you need the funding to do the work that would provide the proof. Parents and friends start to ask how things are going, worried looks stretched across their faces. You count the number of people you've impacted, and it feels small, insignificant. Those moments can feel devastating. But they also are precisely when to remember *why* you are doing this work in the first place. Friends and mentors, part of a successful life, help, too.

In the end, as Seth Godin writes, "persistent people are able to visualize the idea of light at the end of the tunnel when others can't see it." Dips are an inevitable part of life as an agent of change. The key is to use them to enliven and inspire a better future.

"Look, Benje," I said. "You're right. You are a long way from denting Pakistan's broken education system. That work will require a lot of different people, and it still may not happen in your lifetime. But don't get paralyzed thinking about the entire system. Do what you do well. Once you've trained five thousand of those young people—who not only will have good jobs but will demonstrate *character*, practice lifelong learning, and feel part of something bigger than themselves—you will have created a platform. And once you have a platform, you can change the system. But first, build something beautiful." With that, we hugged and each rushed off to our mornings.

When I saw Benje again in 2018, this time in Lahore, he had built a small group of influential Pakistani backers to provide financial support and mentorship, championing Amal's work. Amal Academy had grown into a team of thirty young, driven team members, including ten of their fellowship graduates. The organization had trained thousands of fellows, and forged partnerships with corporations and universities across the country. Benje had started a podcast to spread the message that education is about developing both character and critical thinking skills. He and his business partner, Ali, had become sought-after experts on developing workforces—employees as leaders, as agents of change, rather than workers who simply follow directions. Tens of thousands of lives are different because Benje redefined success for himself, and navigated uncompromisingly toward his north star.

That day in Lahore, I thought of a blogpost Benje had written, sharing sage advice from a mutual friend: "The question isn't just what problem do you want to solve, but how do you want to spend the next forty years of your life?" A couple of years had passed since Benje experienced the Dip. That gentle, brilliant man had become surrounded by erudite young Pakistanis, each of them committed to service and to building their nation from a place of values, with twenty-first-century skills in hand, all of them looking to him as a role model.

* * *

D.light, one of the companies Acumen has supported from its beginning, has brought solar light and electricity to more than one hundred million people across the globe. By all definitions, d.light's founders, Ned Tozun and Sam Goldman (whom I describe further in chapter 4), are successful. But their success goes far beyond the many lives their work has impacted. By tackling one of the world's great challenges, the replacement of kerosene with clean, affordable energy, the company has offset millions of tons of carbon, created jobs for thousands of people who contribute to their nation's development, and laid the groundwork for a new market in off-grid energy.

One of d.light's sales agents is a young woman named Everlyne. I met her in August 2017, in the city of Nakuru, Kenya, as part of a visit to examine some of Acumen's energy investments. Sharply dressed in a black-and-orange, collared d.light shirt, black trousers, and heels, her hair in neat plaits pulled into a ponytail, Everlyne resembled any young professional you might see in any city.

Everlyne confidently guided us on a thirty-minute drive outside the city before stopping by the side of a dirt road. Still in heels, she led us across muddy cornfields until we reached a village that turned out to be hers. She beamed with pride as customers in house after house told us how their lives had changed now that they were able to switch on a light at night, read, talk to their families—in short, do the things most of us take for granted. By the time we left the village, I had no doubt that this young woman was a born salesperson, able to achieve anything she set her mind to doing.

It wasn't until we were in the jeep on our way back to town that Everlyne told her own story of growing up in one of the country's most conservative tribes. "Girls in my community were not permitted to attend schools. But my father was different: he wanted me to study. Because there were no schools for me at home, he sent me to another village to live with my uncle's family and do my schooling. That time in my life was terribly lonely at times, but now I understand that my education meant a difficult life for my father as well: the other men in the village rebuked him for educating me."

I asked her what the men thought of her father's decision now.

"Now they tell their sons to grow up to be like Everlyne."

In redefining success for his daughter, despite the obstacles, Everlyne's father changed the definition of success for the whole village.

"And what do you dream for yourself?" I asked her.

"First, I want to ensure that I bring electricity to every household in my village. I want to serve my community and my country. Once that is done, I want to go to university and study marketing so that I can start my own company."

This African dreamer will not allow herself to focus on individual goals until she fulfills her promise to serve her community.

Thrillingly, there are people like Everlyne in every town and hamlet around the planet.

No matter who you are, the world offers you a thousand opportunities for deeper success. Daily, you might encounter moments to teach the person in front of you as if she herself could change the world, to listen with the reverence that expands the soul of another, to help someone who cannot help himself. At the end of your life, I hope the world says that you cared, that you showed up with your whole self, and that you couldn't have tried harder. I hope they say you helped those who had been left out; that you renewed yourself, living with a sense of curiosity and wonder; learning, changing, and growing till you took your last breath.

In the meantime, we've got a world to change.

Chapter 3

CULTIVATE MORAL
IMAGINATION

About twenty miles east of the Blue Ridge Mountains and home to the University of Virginia, in the early 1980s Charlottesville was a town divided. The locals, many of whom lived in an economically depressed area about a thirty-minute drive from the university, saw the students as rich and privileged. Many locals worked at UVA, where they seemed either invisible to students or served as objects of ridicule, one-dimensional figures with thick Southern mountain accents and humble clothing that separated them from students attired in the requisite Fair Isle sweaters and khaki trousers.

In the fall of my second year at UVA, a popular fraternity threw a huge party asking everyone to dress like a local. The very idea hurt me to think about, and I didn't attend. But I also didn't protest. Then, around Thanksgiving, I chanced upon a flyer inviting students to donate Christmas dinner and toys to a family in need. At least this was an opportunity to do something positive. Inspired, my roommate and I decided to host a holiday party and asked everyone to bring food and a toy.

Our band of friends danced and made merry long into the night. As drinks flowed, a large pile of playthings and food-stuffs burgeoned beneath our scraggly Christmas tree. I went to bed smiling, then rose just a few hours later to pack up my roommate's red car with a veritable Christmas feast, complete with a turkey and all the trimmings, and a big Santa bag full of toys for our "family." We then took off for the edges of town, a bit worse for wear but filled with Christmas spirit and a drive to be of service.

In less than an hour, we arrived in another world: dirt roads and trailer parks, a couple of gas stations, a convenience store with a barely visible street sign. We pulled into one of the gas stations to ask for directions to the family's home. I had trouble understanding the thick accent of the attendant and was mor-tified to ask him to repeat himself, though I wondered whether he had trouble understanding me as well.

Without a road map, my roommate and I managed to lose our bearings a second time. We pulled the car to the side of the road, stopping a man clad in overalls, his head bent downward and his hands in his pockets as he walked along the street. To our request for directions, he responded, "Go down that road till the end." He wore a quizzical expression as he pointed at a dirt road that appeared to lead nowhere. "Take the second left and keep going till you see a sign for Earl's Woodshed. The house is right behind that."

Another few errant turns, past some stray dogs and aban-doned cars, and we finally found a big white sign with "Earl's" written in red. Sure enough, right behind it was a humble shack constructed of slatted wood, with small windows and a porch out front. I stared at the house and suddenly, desperately, hoped no one was home.

Only then did I imagine how our presence might make the family feel. Here we were, two hungover coeds with no connection to this community, arriving from out of nowhere with Christmas in a bag—or at least *our* version of Christmas. Presumably, someone in the family had signed up for this "service," but we knew little about the lives of the people we were hoping to grace with a visit.

And who knew whether they had a clue about us.

A wave of shame engulfed me. "I don't want to meet them," I said.

My roommate looked at me, thought for a moment, and then agreed. With the car still running, I took a deep breath, opened the door, ran as quickly as my legs would carry me, deposited the bags on the porch, and hightailed it back to the car. We then sped off, driving in silence until we found a diner where we could talk about what had just happened.

Our conversation ranged from somber recognition to embarrassed laughter at our own ignorance. We'd sleepwalked into a situation with the best intentions to do something positive for our neighbors, though we'd lived in their city for just over a year and they'd been there forever. We were glad to bring fresh food and toys to a family that might otherwise have gone without, but this kind of drive-by charity felt wrong somehow, for everyone.

Years later, I've thought about what I might say to my younger self about that long-ago day. I would commend the instinct to make a contribution, however small. But well-meaning acts of kindness are not enough. I would push my younger self to move from the blanket statement "I want to help disadvantaged people" to visualizing herself in the shoes of those she wanted to serve.

This is where moral imagination begins. But it doesn't stop there.

Moral imagination means to view other people's problems as if they were your own, and to begin to discern how to tackle those problems. And then to act accordingly. It summons us to understand and transcend the realities of current circumstances and to envision a better future for ourselves and others.

Moral imagination starts with empathy, but it does not content itself simply to feel another's pain. Empathy without action risks reinforcing the status quo. Rather, moral imagination is muscular, built from the bottom up and grounded through immersion in the lives of others. It involves connecting on a human level, analyzing the systemic issues at play, and only then envisioning how to go beyond applying a Band-Aid to making a long-term difference.

Moral imagination is the basis of an ethical framework for a world that recognizes our common humanity and insists on opportunity, choice, and dignity for all of us. Had I approached the Christmas food and toy drive with moral imagination, I might have started by learning about the community and the realities those who lived there faced. If I couldn't spend time with the families we wanted to serve, I could at least have asked for information beyond just the children's genders and ages, which was the only data provided. And I might have tried to connect with the family beforehand, ensuring even the barest of relationships. I could even have asked to meet just the parents, so as not to risk spoiling the children's dreams of a magical Santa-delivered Christmas.

Listening to voices unheard, a value I discuss in the next

chapter, is fundamental to the moral imagination. So is gathering knowledge about those we intend to serve. If my roommate and I were unwilling to gain such knowledge, I should have found an organization with a long-term commitment to the community and supported it so that it could do a better job than we could do ourselves.

The world has changed dramatically in the thirty years since that winter day in the Blue Ridge Mountains. For one, technological advances have given us GPS, so that we rarely have to ask for directions. And the divide between classes has become a chasm. For the privileged, everything seems possible: sending spaceships and inhabiting Mars, enhancing human capabilities by merging with robots, living forever. But this world of infinite possibility and space travel can seem impossibly distant to those who feel irrelevant, vulnerable, or just plain poor. And if the demise of easily automated, repetitive work engenders dreams of growing creative endeavors for the highly educated, the end of stable employment may feel understandably precarious for those without university degrees.

What is needed, whether you are working in high tech or in low-income communities, is the *moral imagination* to ensure that our future solutions and institutions are inclusive and sustainable. That takes a particular kind of capability, one driven by empathy, immersion, connection, and the willingness to challenge the status quo.

One of the great privileges of my life is to work with remarkable individuals whose leadership is grounded in moral imagination. Gayathri Vasudevan of Bangalore, India, is one of them, though I wouldn't have guessed that when I first heard about her company, LabourNet.

In 2012, Acumen decided to invest in education, but we

were having a hard time finding financially viable investment candidates. A colleague suggested LabourNet, which already had trained more than a hundred thousand workers. I was skeptical: I'd seen hundreds of millions of aid dollars spent on vocational training and "technical assistance" (nonfinancial training provided by consultants, usually), most of it wasted. Such programs tended to be poorly run, with little focus on training workers in the skills that hiring companies actually needed. That said, I'd not yet encountered Gayathri Vasudevan, who, I would discover, defined herself not by the size of her budget but by the changed lives of those she served.

I met Gayathri on a construction site just outside Bangalore in December 2014. LabourNet had undertaken a contract to train workers there, and Gayathri planned to introduce me to some of her trainees. Dressed in a black-and-gold silk sari, her salt-and-pepper hair in a pragmatic bob tucked beneath a bright orange construction hat, she cut a memorable figure.

I laughed. "Do you wear beautiful saris to every construction site?"

"Why not?" she responded with a smile that was at once self-effacing and mischievous. "I wear saris daily. They are just a part of who I am."

I was glad Gayathri didn't feel she had to be anyone but herself. "Then, how did a nice girl like you end up in a place like this?" I replied with a laugh, sensing already that I could go beyond political correctness and be myself as well. "I'd love to hear your story."

"For the first three years of my career, I lived in remote rural villages," she began. "I was always interested in policy reform for India, but I couldn't bear the thought of trying to influence policies from the safe perch of an office. I needed to understand on-the-ground realities."

Now Gayathri was singing my song. First step: immersion.

"You know, Jacqueline," she said, "I had my own arrogant assumptions when I lived in the villages. I thought the poor could solve their problems through entrepreneurship alone. But spending time with people in their own environments showed me a different reality. The most vulnerable people tend to be risk averse: when you live at the edge of survival, life itself can be a risky proposition. The poor value the stability and predictability of a consistent job. Most people, wealthy or poor, want to avoid the potential windfalls and painful losses associated with entrepreneurship."

Gayathri continued: "Over the next decades, I also witnessed well-educated Indians gain lucrative jobs in the tech sector while three hundred million untrained, unskilled, uneducated people were left behind with little attention focused on them." Armed with enhanced understanding, Gayathri set out to reimagine a better system. She and her cofounder, Rajesh AR, started LabourNet to take on the massive problem of India's unskilled and underemployed, which includes 90 percent of the workforce. She was realistic about the rise of automation, among other challenges, but it hurt her to see employers treat untrained workers as merely replaceable inputs.

As in many countries, the informal sector in India exists beyond the realm of regulation or taxation. Informal laborers may be self-employed street vendors, beauticians, domestic workers, personal service providers, mechanics, bricklayers, tailors, and the like, or they may work for the subcontractors that form an increasingly complex web of the global economy. These workers stitch fabric for hours at a stretch; toil over vats of lye in leather tanneries, inhaling toxic fumes without gloves and masks; or labor as bar benders, ironworkers, or cement mixers, forgoing personal safety on hazardous half-built construction sites.

These are the people too often hidden in the basement of a global marketplace that demands faster, cheaper goods. They are the invisible, the nobodies—and there are more of them all the time. A constant wave of entrants into India's labor economy, nearly twenty million people a year, makes this precarious situation even worse for those who see no choice but to accept low-status, low-wage jobs at high risk to their health and, sometimes, their lives.

Consequently, Gayathri has focused her attention on giving informal workers opportunities to imagine and then build more predictable futures with some potential for upward mobility. Doing this required training and supporting workers with the skills to help them navigate an unstructured, unstable informal labor market. To achieve this, she built structures where few existed.

"Shall we go up?" she asked, gesturing to a rickety bamboo ladder nearby. We ambled up it, reaching the exposed second floor of the concrete behemoth before walking across an open platform, past pillars and piles of concrete blocks, until we saw a wooden door with the LabourNet logo on it.

Inside, in a small room, forty or so young men, most of whom looked like schoolboys except for the telltale clothing of their trade (jeans, neon orange vests, and bright blue or yellow hard hats) sat five to a bench in front of skinny tables. The construction workers fixed their eyes on Gayathri, who walked to the front of the room and greeted the men with a smile as they stood to welcome her. Gayathri then proceeded to give a pep talk in Hindi, a second language to most of these men, who had come from the far reaches of the country. She told the men that it was up to them to build skills that could lead to more control over their lives. I couldn't help but reflect on the fact that these men were earning so little, living so far away from their homes, working on a structure that would soon house million-dollar apartments because of their sweat.

"Is this training really enough to change the workers' lives?" I asked Gayathri after her lecture. And then I added—lightly, for I know there must be days when this heroic woman is daunted by the sea of unemployed young people rising monthly—"or will the system inevitably grind them down?"

Instead of answering, she suggested we speak with the men themselves. A nineteen-year-old with dark brown eyes and a fringe of black hair pushing out of his blue hat, smartphone in hand, spoke confidently of all he'd learned. "The training is an important start," he said. "At home, I couldn't take care of my family from the farm's income. Now I send enough money for my children to attend schools. I want my children to have better lives than I did. I want to make them proud."

"How far away from your family do you live now?" I asked.

"Maybe two thousand kilometers," he responded—a four-day trip each way, if all goes well.

The earnest worker reminded me of my grandfather, who immigrated to Pennsylvania from Austria as a young man, married at twenty, and hauled ninety-pound bags of cement each day to give his six children the chance for a life he was not lucky enough to have. I thought, too, about the correlation between the right kind of training and the confidence it imparts. LabourNet's ethos requires reinforcing in every worker the notion that they are important enough for someone to invest in them. Only when we dare to believe that our future can be different do we have a chance of making it so.

I wished the young man every success.

As I write this, LabourNet has trained more than seven

hundred thousand workers in fields ranging from construction to automotive repair to tailoring. Yet, Gayathri believes this training alone is not enough. From among the workers Labour-Net educates, her team identifies those who are interested in entrepreneurial opportunities, and then reaches out to help develop their ideas. The company has already enabled more than seven thousand people to start their own companies. I've met several of these entrepreneurs, each of whom employs at least ten people. LabourNet supports them, mitigating the risks of entrepreneurship by connecting them with large companies that need their services, whether they sew school uniforms or distribute beauty products. In essence, the company extends its "social capital," or networks of connections, to low-resourced but well-trained entrepreneurial individuals who can, in turn, provide vital services and finally earn levels of income that are commensurate with their efforts.

By immersing herself in the realities of low-income laborers and using her moral imagination, Gayathri came to understand the larger system of workforce development. As her understanding and effectiveness grew, she gained legitimacy and a voice that enabled her to advocate for worker-oriented policies. LabourNet has influenced skills certification and performance standards in a number of sectors such as automobile, leather, and infrastructure. The company has also played a role in prodding the Indian government to include vocational training as part of the country's national education curriculum. Over time, Gayathri has become a national voice for the unheard. Her work is an example of moral imagination in action.

* * *

From urban India to post-conflict Colombia, moral imagination is providing a springboard to creative solutions that acknowledge the vulnerable and respect our natural resources. The steps that effective, pragmatic, idealistic change agents take, from empathy to action, tend to be the same, regardless of how or where each story begins.

In 2009, Carlos Ignacio Velasco, a soft-spoken, whip-smart young Colombian working as a representative of his country's coffee industry in Tokyo, met Mayumi Ogata, a passionate chocolate connoisseur who had just completed a four-year pursuit to identify the world's finest varieties of cacao.

After working for years in a premium chocolate company, Mayumi had wearied of the toll the industry took on farmers and the earth. More than 90 percent of the world's chocolate is produced by about five million smallholder families, 90 percent of whom earn less than two dollars per day. And 70 percent of cacao is cultivated in West Africa, often through unsustainable farming methods that have worn down the soil. Faced with these alarming statistics, Mayumi sought new areas where high-quality varieties of the cacao fruit could be cultivated more profitably for the farmers and without harming the planet.

Of the many places she'd visited, from Indonesia to Bolivia, Colombia ultimately captured Mayumi's heart. There, she found diverse, delicate varieties of cacao in a number of regions. But these same regions also had suffered a half century of civil war, and still bore wounds from the violence of drug lords, FARC (Revolutionary Armed Forces of Colombia) guerrillas, and paramilitaries. The lands rich in cacao also are geographically isolated from Colombia's main cities, and education and skills levels are quite low. Despite the risks, Mayumi assessed that prospects for cacao production were phenomenal there. Besides, she loved a challenge.

Carlos had already been thinking about what more he could do to contribute to his country: those early meetings with Mayumi in Tokyo set his imagination alight. If Colombia could be known for some of the best coffee beans on earth, he wondered, why couldn't it also build a world-class chocolate industry? After all, coffee was introduced to Colombia from Ethiopia in the nineteenth century. Cacao, on the other hand, was part of the region's natural inheritance.

Moreover, the post-conflict areas of the country needed deliberate investment in the land and its people if peace were to flourish. What better way to contribute than to build a company that would produce some of the world's finest cacao in partnership with local communities? Here, Carlos believed, was a chance to demonstrate the power of business, if infused with moral imagination, to produce not just profits for the few, but prosperity and peace where communities had for too long felt abandoned.

Carlos and Mayumi cofounded Cacao de Colombia that same year, 2009, and began to work on building trusted relationships with farmers' groups in four different post-conflict regions. This process would take years, but time plus conscious effort infused with moral imagination enables possibility.

In 2017, two years into Acumen's investment in Cacao de Colombia, I had the privilege of visiting a farming community in the Sierra Nevada de Santa Marta, one of the highest coastal mountain ranges on earth, located in Colombia's far north. There lie the ancestral lands of the Arhuacos, an indigenous people known for their commitment to living in harmony with the universe. In those mountains, Mayumi had come upon an exquisite rare white cacao guaranteed to produce some of the world's finest chocolate. She and Carlos dreamed of forming a partnership with the Arhuacos to produce a world-class chocolate and export a philosophy, not just a product, to the rest of the world.

It was certainly not a given that the Arhuacos would be interested. They had kept their traditions intact despite terrors imposed by colonizers, drug dealers, and soldiers. And they considered the white cacao a sacred fruit, no longer cultivated or commercialized. Greed-oriented capitalism posed a new threat. Carlos and Mayumi would therefore have to earn the Arhuacos' trust, designing a transformative partnership—and that took time. The work required starting with an understanding of local history, customs, and values before proceeding with mutual respect.

As Acumen's Latin America director, Virgilio Barco, and I drove with Mayumi along Colombia's coast to our meeting point with the Arhuacos, I asked Mayumi how the partnership had been built. How had she and Carlos and the Arhuacos weighed what would be gained and what would be lost by partnering to grow and commercialize the rare cacao?

Mayumi spoke about the spirituality of the Arhuacos, who believe in the interconnection of all living things. "I feel a resonance with this idea," she said. "I was raised with Shintoism in Japan. We also see the connection between ourselves and the natural world. Between my own belief system and the Arhuacos', I can count more than eight hundred divinities inspired by water, wind, and earth. I respond to their spiritualism. I respond to their worldview. Our mutual understanding helped build trust. They could feel both my respect and my connection to them."

A spiritual connection is one way to transcend lines of difference and locate commonality. Mayumi and Carlos could also have connected based on other strands of their identities (their love of nature, their commitment to learning), but for Mayumi especially, spiritual bonds created the basis for her deep curiosity and respect.

We arrived at a modest village nestled by the pale blue sea where it greets a sudden rise of green, towering mountains. I thought to myself: No wonder the Arhuacos believe this place to be the center of the universe.

Mamo Camilo, a spiritual leader, and several of his associates welcomed us warmly and guided us to sit with them beneath a tree. The Arhuacos wear simple, homespun white tunics and loosely fitted trousers. The men's long black hair cascades out of their white woven caps, which symbolize the snow-capped peaks of the sacred mountains. Mamo Camilo, distinguished and serene, though undifferentiated in dress, clearly garnered the respect of the other Arhuacos, who made way for him when he walked by and hung on his words when he spoke.

The *mamos* (wise guides) exert powerful influence within Arhuaco communities. Selected as boys, they train for a decade, learning the philosophy of the Arhuacos, along with traditional medicinal practices and the arts of listening and arbitrating differences among people. The day I first visited the Arhuacos with Carlos and Mayumi, the *mamos* spent three hours with us, providing a master class in the Arhuaco cosmology. The Arhuacos believe that nature and society are united by a single immutable law of the universe that has always existed and always will, even after human beings have left the planet.

"We see your culture as the world's little brother," Mamo Camilo said, with no trace of scolding. "Your people think the land is for their pleasure alone. Ours is a philosophy that must grow with maturity. We the Arhuacos are the elder brothers. We come with understanding that we must respect all living creatures of the earth. We seek harmony. Now the land has given us the rarest cacao, and it is to all of us to nurture and ensure its preservation."

As Mamo Camilo expounded on the cosmology of the Arhuacos, he modeled something else: how to own your power. His confidence and worldview were essential components of his negotiations. Though economically "poorer," his community was arguably richer in spirit and happiness. And he understood that the Arhuacos had something to give—not just materially, but in terms of their philosophy. After acknowledging and affirming the respectful way in which Carlos and Mayumi had entered negotiations, Mamo Camilo shared some of his worries about partnering with those who operate in a modern capitalist system. What happens to the earth if we see it as a resource but not a responsibility?

As we walked back toward the village center together, I noticed some of the young men holding cell phones. I wondered aloud how the tribe ultimately would draw the line between needs and wants, and whether entering a contract with the company might open a Pandora's box of temptations.

"We understand that we cannot live in the past," Mamo Camilo said. "To survive, we must engage with the larger world. Today, our people need phones if they are going to interact with others beyond the Arhuacos. We need a few other essential things, like batteries and solar lights. And we need to continually remind ourselves of our responsibility for the earth."

Then he added that they would not have made a deal with anyone but Cacao de Colombia, because of an earned mutual respect, but he added a caveat: "We will partner only so long as our project does not disturb our balance with nature. If we lose the balance, we will end the partnership. Do you understand?"

"Yes," I said. I believed I did.

This was a negotiation based not on extraction or profit alone. The agreement between the Arhuacos and the company was more covenant than contract, a moral commitment to remaining accountable to each other, to showing up, to listening. Spending immersive time together had enabled each side to understand what the other needed in order for the relationship to work. For the Arhuacos, participation with the company was a means to sustaining their community, enabling it to continue transmitting its ancestral wisdom to benefit humanity. For Cacao de Colombia, it was the opportunity to build a successful business that valued human and natural resources, not only financial rewards. Both community and company will be changed by the partnership, just as any relationship of equals changes both partners over time.

As the company grows and the Arhuacos become wealthier as a tribe, pressures to conform to "business as usual" and cut corners or demand faster growth will inevitably increase. Finding values-aligned investors steeped in their own moral imagination will be key. But had the company's founders not dared first to imagine what could be, Cacao de Colombia would never have gotten started.

In 2018, the International Chocolate Awards, honoring the best chocolates in the world, gave Arhuaco chocolates gold and silver medals in the Single Bean and Micro-Batch categories. This achievement was possible because of a Shinto-observing Japanese cacao whisperer; a Catholic-raised, Shinto-aspiring Colombian entrepreneur; and an indigenous community adhering to a philosophy based on oneness with the cosmos. Each had the moral imagination to extend a hand to those who were different, seeking what united them and bonding in purpose.

Moral imagination offers a powerful lens through which to see the world's potential, recognize its disparities, and work to address them. Use it widely and practice it wisely.

Chapter 4

LISTEN TO VOICES
UNHEARD

On a Sunday afternoon in 2015, I sat with my colleague Bavidra Mohan in one of India's thousands of red-and-white Coffee Day shops. This one was on the corner of Carter Road in Bandra, a trendy suburb in the western part of Mumbai. We'd arranged a meeting with Vimal Kumar, newly elected to the Acumen Fellowship in India. But it was a quarter past the hour, with no sign of Vimal. I'd usually attribute such tardiness to Mumbai traffic, but this was a Sunday.

I knew little about Vimal then, except that he hailed from the same low caste, the scavengers, as the women Ankit employed to transform temple flowers into incense and other products. Unlike the women, who felt relatively voiceless before working for Ankit, Vimal was an established community leader with a megaphone. He was an activist founder of the Movement for Scavenger Community, a grassroots Indian NGO focused on improving conditions for scavengers and standing for the rights of all people. He was also earning a PhD, which seemed a Herculean achievement to me. I wanted to understand what obstacles Vimal had overcome, and how he had integrated his many facets. There was much the world could learn from a man like him, if he first understood himself.

The longer we waited at the coffee shop, the more I wondered if Vimal might be waiting for us outside. Had I missed him on my way in? The privileged tend to take for granted our right to enter most places, including department stores, banks, elite universities, upscale restaurants, or even lines at immigration counters. For those who have been shunned repeatedly, however, or even "politely" informed that their kind doesn't "fit," nothing is taken for granted. Though already a man of many accomplishments, Vimal, accustomed to being unseen and unheard, experienced "the rules" differently than I did.

I left the coffee shop and, sure enough, found him standing outside, dressed in a yellow shirt and long trousers, his face moist with sweat. I could have recognized him from photos I'd seen of his broad, open face, his penetrating eyes and dark hair parted neatly on the side. But his smile was a dead giveaway.

"Hello, Vimal!" I said enthusiastically. He extended his hand. I was unprepared for his soft, gentle grasp. Instinctively, I pulled him into a hug, and was struck again by his tentativeness. "Let's go inside and get out of the heat," I said, and he smiled in agreement. As we were walking into the cafe, I asked him what he'd like to drink and eat. I pointed to the glass cabinets of croissants, muffins, and sandwiches. Vimal insisted that all he wanted was water.

Back at our table, Bavidra and I mostly listened as Vimal shared stories of his childhood. He counted himself among the lucky ones. Boys and girls from his caste were typically denied education and rejected by schools. Sometimes parents' own fears—of rejection or failure—were enough to keep children out of school.

Vimal said he considered himself fortunate to have a mother who wanted desperately for him to learn what had not been available to her. She cleaned the toilets at a good private school whose headmaster allowed Vimal to attend classes—provided he sit in the back of the classroom. And though he loved learning, Vimal endured a lonely separateness from the rest of the boys. Everyone knew he was considered "untouchable," and his status was made more visible by the fact that he could afford only patched, ragged clothes, in sharp contrast to the school uniforms worn by the other students.

As he grew, so did his anger at the injustice of a system that would deny his people the opportunities considered normal for everyone else. When the first cable company came to his area, everyone got access to satellite TV except for those belonging to his caste. Vimal responded by organizing a group of local boys to tear down every installed satellite dish. When the company replaced the satellites, Vimal, now a street fighter, tore them down again, promising to continue the cycle until the company agreed to serve scavengers.

"We weren't asking for any favors," he said. "We just wanted the chance to pay like everyone else."

When the company agreed to make the satellite dishes available to everyone, Vimal felt vindicated. Though he wasn't proud of an approach that involved the destruction of property, he internalized that the powerless can sometimes engage the powerful and "win."

I said that our fellowship focused on nonviolent approaches to change, yet acknowledged that history is full of incidences of violence and wars fought by frustrated, resentful young men with few reasons to hope for their futures. Vimal admitted that part of him was still motivated by anger.

"Angry with the system in general?" I asked, "or with specific groups of people?"

"I'm angry that so many people believed India's problems were solved when caste was supposedly abolished. I'm angry that my community is denied opportunities for reasons that have nothing to do with our abilities and everything to do with the circumstances of our birth."

I could feel Vimal seething as he spoke, though there also was something so gentle about him. I imagined the warring parts of himself, his own bull and dove, the side that could take on the world versus the side still battling the weight of trauma and stigma. Where might he be complicit in holding himself back? What beautiful parts from his life experiences might he bring forth to offer the world? How could our community help him unleash his potential?

"What are you going to do with all that anger?" I asked.

"I'm going to fight for change," he said.

As we were leaving, Vimal thanked me for hugging him when we first met. "This is the first time in my life," he said, "when I have met someone new and been welcomed as a friend rather than interrogated as a stranger." He went on to say that Acumen was the first organization he'd encountered where people actually physically touched him.

I was elevated by this opportunity to listen to Vimal across so many generational layers of structures and traditions intended to marginalize people like him. I felt humbled by his humility and elated that he was now part of our community. Yet, though I consider myself a good listener, I realized only later that I heard only his *emotional* hunger that day, and failed to hear what Vimal could not say, failed to recognize how *physically* hungry he was. As we were in a simple coffee shop and Vimal was officially part of our fellowship, I had unmindfully assumed that when I asked Vimal if he wanted food or drink, he'd give me an honest reply, knowing that I would pay and that the bill would not set me back much. What the poet Seamus Heaney would call my "creeping privilege"* collided with Vimal's utter lack of entitlement.

A few years after our first visit, Vimal admitted that he had waited outside for me because he had no money in his pocket. What if a server had asked him to buy a coffee or a pastry? The thought of being seen as a loiterer panicked him. Then, when I asked him if he wanted something to drink or eat, he feared I might later request that he split the bill. Though he'd not eaten in many hours, pride, or shame, overtook his hunger.

Privilege can deafen us to those who feel less worthy or valuable. Those for whom the system "works" can easily become accustomed to the world rolling out a welcome mat and learn to behave as if every place were our exclusive domain.

Meanwhile, outsiders or those deemed "other," who've been told repeatedly that they are unworthy or don't belong, often internalize negative beliefs imposed on them by others and make themselves smaller, unable to give voice to their true feelings, opinions, or desires. If we want to see someone more fully and demonstrate that we respect him or her, we must learn to listen not just with our ears, but with all of our selves—our eyes, the emotion we sense in the other, our knowledge of their history, of their very identity. Listening deeply and hearing all that is unsaid is crucial to gaining awareness of self and of others.

It was another year before I had the chance to talk directly

---

* From the poem "From the Republic of Conscience."

with Vimal again. The time seemed to have changed him. His unassuming smile was still there, but the anger was gone. He described the various seminars he had attended, how in the early Acumen Fellows sessions he'd start every conversation by throwing a figurative punch.

"I kept trying to fight," he said. "I didn't know how to be any other way. But none of the fellows would fight back. Finally, I had to recognize that the other fellows were genuinely interested in what I had to say. They wanted to know me. When I finally paid enough attention to accept their interest, to accept *myself*, I in turn wanted to listen more to them."

If privilege is a possible roadblock to deep listening, so is clinging rigidly to an outsider identity. We risk holding ourselves hostage to outdated stories of being unwanted or underappreciated, failing to hear even direct invitations to the proverbial table as an equal participant. Only when Vimal allowed himself to believe that the other fellows saw him as part of themselves could he in turn see those same people as part of him. When individual listening is ingrained in collective culture, the whole community is more likely to shine.

Empowered by a sense of belonging and acceptance, Vimal began to expand his trust to people beyond the group, slowly taking greater risks. While running his organization on behalf of the scavenger community and studying for his PhD, he also started consulting on questions of diversity for companies such as Microsoft. He broadened his view of the world, standing for issues related both to his caste and to other marginalized groups.

A few months later, in 2016, Vimal and I met again in Mumbai, this time at the tail end of a weeklong Acumen trip across India with a group of donors (or partners, as we call them). My team wanted the group to meet not only with Acumen investee companies, but also with the fellows, both to understand the purpose of supporting such a diverse cohort of emerging leaders and, we hoped, to forge new friendships and reinforce the idea of a single community bound by shared values.

The Friday afternoon sun was bright as about ten partners and ten fellows gathered in Acumen's offices, a light-filled space above a major thoroughfare in Bandra. The office windows, covered with shades in Acumen's colors (fuchsia, lime green, violet, and royal blue), overlooked a handful of trees, though you could hear the sounds of auto-rickshaws and cars jamming the streets below. The partners and fellows were there to practice deep listening.

In an exercise inspired by the nonprofit oral history project StoryCorps, we paired each partner with a fellow and sent them on a walk along Carter Road, a path that winds along the Arabian Sea. We hoped the chance to look outward while moving side by side would soften edges and enable more intimate exchanges.

Each duo was instructed to walk for half an hour as one person listened to the other's story (twenty minutes of sharing, then ten minutes for questions); they would exchange the roles on the walk back. A Swedish filmmaker accompanied an Indian woman engineer; an American business leader walked alongside an Indian schoolteacher. The goal was to discover not what made them different, but what they shared.

Back at the office, the group reunited. The air felt electric. A number of attendees remarked on the rare gift of having someone give you their undivided attention. Active listening, we agreed, is one of the deepest forms of respect.

I asked each person to introduce his or her partner, emphasizing any common ground they had uncovered. We had paired Vimal with the American social psychologist Jonathan Haidt, whose work focused on how we speak to one another, in part because they were both so interested in the role of culture in society. And as they were chatting happily when they rejoined the group, I calculated that they would be a good duo to kick off the discussion.

Jonathan offered to start. He smiled as he referenced the good fortune of meeting Vimal, but his voice became more serious as he spoke. "I know I'm supposed to talk about all that Vimal and I share," he said. "But truthfully, our lives have little in common. I grew up in a privileged environment as a well-educated American. My parents gave me every opportunity and every advantage. My children have even more privilege.

"Vimal," he continued, "has had to fight disadvantage his entire life. His mother carried human waste in a basket on her head, cleaning the village and finally the school. Vimal was allowed to attend classes, but his mother had no idea how isolated he was. When he was eight years old, she invited her son's entire class to their home to celebrate Vimal's birthday. She cleaned and cooked for two whole days, all the while imagining the joy her little boy would feel with his friends celebrating him. But they waited all day, and not a single student showed up."

Jonathan's eyes welled with tears. "I have an eight-year-old son, and I can't bear the thought of what it would mean for him to be in a similar situation. No, you see, Vimal and I aren't alike. My life has been so easy in comparison."

Vimal reached over, putting his arm on Jonathan's shoulder.

"No, Jon," Vimal softly admonished, "there is much that we share. You love India. I love India. We both have studied marginal groups. We both have two children. Plus, you are a Jew. You know what it means to be persecuted for no reason other than something you were born into being. You know how unfair and unproductive that is." He paused.

"And besides"—now Vimal smiled—"we both have PhDs."

When we dare to meet another as a friend, willing to hear painful and uncomfortable truths, we can discover the parts of our identities that overlap. We can acknowledge the other person's—and our own—yearning to be seen. True listening is more than the act of hearing another's words. It is the unspoken recognition of our shared humanity.

Today, we exchange more words with one another than at any time in history. Yet how many people are really listening? Not only are we distracted by our devices, but we see leaders everywhere doing everything *but* listening, becoming louder and shriller in their arguments. With those who seem opposed to our views, we can be especially like strangers, acting as if those who speak a different language should easily understand our words. Our hearts and our heads are divided at precisely the time when we most need them to work in tandem.

Those in positions of authority—anyone whose words might carry greater weight than the voices of others—need to listen more, and not assume that because the rules work for them, they know what works for everyone. Yet I've also witnessed nonprofit leaders and entrepreneurs undervalue the experience and knowledge of donors and investors based on their own narrow assumptions.

Listening effectively can influence the way we perceive others *in all directions*. Just as being poor says nothing about a person's character, neither does the bank account that marks someone as rich. In the world of fund-raising, I've witnessed grant or investment seekers categorically write off the person who failed to approve their request rather than take the time to listen to the former's constructive feedback. Strategically, as my friend and founding Acumen board member Stuart

Davidson says, "If you want advice, ask for money. If you want to raise money, ask for advice." We all yearn to be recognized.

Markets, too, can be a powerful listening device, efficiently allocating resources to places where customers are saying most clearly, "We want this." Think of it this way. If I offer you a gift, how likely are you to turn it down, even if it doesn't quite meet your needs? But what if I treat you as a customer? You and I might haggle over the price, but as the seller, I will know a lot more about your likes and dislikes, about where you want to spend your resources, than if you were simply a passive recipient of my benevolent intentions.

Yet markets fail the poor, especially those who lack enough income to meet even basic needs. When it comes to health care, education, drinking water, or housing, low-income people desperate to address critical needs may have no choice other than turning to moneylenders or mafias for loans, often at usurious rates. The poor must accept prices that are many times what the middle class or wealthy might ever be required to pay. And though well-intentioned charities might step in, seeing the pain points of the poor, these nonprofits often bring the services they *believe* low-income people need rather than the services the poor truly require. Few stop to listen to what the poor actually want, causing those in need to get stuck between the cheats and the charities, their problems often multiplying as a result.

It doesn't have to be this way. A growing group of social entrepreneurs is turning conventional models of capitalism upside down and reimagining business from the perspective not only of the wealthy, but specifically, of the vulnerable. These entrepreneurs start by listening to the poor with the understanding that we can solve our problems if we begin by treating low-income people not as passive recipients of charity but as customers who desire and deserve a greater sense of agency to make their own decisions and chart the courses of their own lives.

Consider the issue of electricity. Thomas Edison developed the incandescent lightbulb in 1879 and commercialized its production the following year. It has been more than 140 years, and nearly a billion people on earth still have no access to electricity. On the African continent alone, more than six hundred million people live in darkness once the sun goes down, losing productivity and security as well as a thousand other things the rest of us take for granted.

Energy poverty, as the gap in global electricity is called, is not just a market failure. It is a moral failure. The world possesses the technology, the know-how, and the financial resources to solve the challenge of universal electricity. Our individual and collective will has been the single most important impediment to lighting the world. But this is slowly changing as a small group of social entrepreneurs combine exciting new clean-energy technologies with financially sustainable business models that have opened a path to electrifying homes of the poor while helping to avert long-term climate crisis. The best of these of models are grounded in values of listening and paying attention to behaviors of low-income people as well as their words.

All people desire at least some level of light, and all require a heat source for cooking. Most low-income Africans still depend on kerosene-fueled hurricane lamps, a technology America and Europe ditched a century ago. Though a ten-billion-dollar market, kerosene as an energy source is dirty, dangerous, and expensive, but that market has remained strong because there have been no good, affordable, accessible kerosene alternatives available to the poor.

There are structural and practical reasons that kerosene remains in widespread use. First, households are able to acquire it in tiny amounts. In Kenya, for instance, the average low-income household spends about forty cents a day to light a hurricane lantern in the evenings. If a family falls on hard times, they can skip a night or two of light and purchase more when better times return. Second, because such small amounts are sold at a time, merchants build in a very high profit margin. Mafias, or predatory businesses, control access to kerosene and often have strong ties to local government officials. These officials use tax dollars to subsidize the price of kerosene for low-income people in exchange for votes. Kerosene is therefore widely available, and often the only option a poor household has. It provides energy for light, but at a high cost to the individual in terms of income, health, and quality of life.

However, despite ingrained hurdles, any system can change if we care enough. Sam Goldman and Ned Tozun are two entrepreneurs determined to reject the status quo that has kept more than 1.5 billion people dependent on kerosene. And they know how to listen.

Raised in a household of aid workers, Sam grew up mostly in the developing world playing with boys and girls who, though woefully lacking in opportunity, wanted to do the same things he did. After university, he lived in an unelectrified village in Benin, West Africa, as a Peace Corps volunteer. He saved money by wearing a small LED headlamp at night so that he could read and go to the outdoor latrine without suffering the effects of the expensive, smoky kerosene that wreaked havoc on his neighbors.

"For years, I accepted that a state of darkness went hand in hand with village life," he once told me. Until, one night, a kerosene lantern toppled over in his neighbor's home, burning down the house and severely injuring the eldest son.

Sam decided to do something. He began by writing to a number of companies that sold portable lights, hoping he might become a distributor. No one responded. His next move was to apply to Stanford Business School with the intention of learning how to start the company he could not yet find. There, he met Ned, an engineer who had recently worked in Malawi recording the stories of AIDS victims. He, too, wanted to start a business that would empower the poor. Both Ned and Sam understood the system that kept people in poverty as it was, but they focused instead on what could be done to change it.

Many young entrepreneurs might have been overwhelmed by the complicated dynamics of low-income markets. The most economically disadvantaged live in places dominated by vested interests engaged in the "industry" of poverty—not just local mafias, but local politicians, who often have a personal stake in controlling the funds allocated for a community or region; religious leaders; and even mothers-in-law who often prefer to maintain their own privileged status within a social system that, though broken for most people, works for them. But in such a corrupt and complicated system, there is almost no top-down way to solve a problem like electricity access.

From the start, Ned and Sam's entrepreneurial advantage was embedded in their experiences in Africa and their respect for the poor as customers. They started small and listened closely, all the while imagining the world they hoped to create. While still at Stanford, they developed a single prototype for a solar-powered lantern.

In 2007 when Sam and Ned first brought their idea to my team at Acumen, we didn't have a lot to work with. Their business plan for a company called d.light rested on their assumption that they could sell their lantern for thirty dollars, the two reasoning that if the average household paid about forty cents daily for kerosene, it would take them less than three months to save up for the lamp. The young entrepreneurs had built some networks, but it was their character that ultimately convinced Acumen to invest. Our intuition told us that they were seekers like us, driven by the right ideals and prepared to back those up with grit.

The d.light founders listened right from the outset. They asked their customers for ways to improve the product itself—though at first they learned very little. Real listening is not a one-time event. If you want to build a solution for a group that has traditionally had no voice, be prepared to listen continuously. It may take you longer than you think to hear what people are actually saying, especially when they have no reason to trust you.

Of course, Ned and Sam made mistakes and found themselves in dead ends—for years. That is the price of building an entirely new market. While, theoretically, low-income people could pay off a thirty-dollar light over three months, given the precariousness of their lives, they could not save enough to meet the monthly payments. And even if they loved the product, most of them had doubts about this newfangled way of lighting their homes. Why should they risk their hard-earned money on something that might break in a month? Few had seen a product like this in the marketplace. Better to stay with something they knew.

Sam and Ned took failure in stride, listening for clues as to what might succeed. They knew they would have to work harder to earn trust. Building a company infused with purpose was the founders' antidote to wariness. That meant inculcating in every employee a definition of success based on more than just selling whatever they could to earn a day's income; this company was going to light the world.

And every employee needed to believe in that vision and internalize it. They had to treat every potential customer with deep respect, showing up repeatedly, asking questions, and listening to people, even if they didn't like what they had to say. In time, d.light began to earn customers, and the company learned to build real relationships.

I remember, years later, when d.light had become an established company, sitting in a rural hut in central Kenya with an unlikely trio: Teresia, a pint-size grandmother; her sweet one-year-old grandson, on her lap; and David, a burly Australian with a shock of white hair, the company's Africa director. We were there because Teresia and her daughter had purchased one of the lanterns a few months prior, and we wanted to hear her impressions.

Teresia's face—calm, lined, square—make me think of my Austrian grandmother, who also grew up on a rural farm and knew the sweat of hard work. Though Teresia lived in a small house that could feel like midnight inside in the middle of the day, she lit up as she turned on her solar lantern, telling us how it had changed her life, how even during daily brownouts in her village, when the grid stopped working, she was still able to see.

"So, how could the company improve the light?" I asked.

She hesitated for a second, then placed her hand on her hip, cocked her head to the side, and spoke directly to David. "It would be good if the light could charge the cell phone while charging itself as well," she said. I smiled at the glint in her eye, the seriousness of her intent. I'd witnessed so many encounters in which well-intentioned charities asked people if they appreciated the services delivered and, inevitably, the beneficiaries nodded their heads and told them all was well.

But this time, Teresia was giving *us* advice. We were listening to her, and not the other way around.

I thanked her for her good comments.

She responded by raising her eyebrow and giving me a look to indicate that she was not finished making suggestions.

I loved it.

"Two," she continued, "you know, batteries for the radio are too expensive. We couldn't listen to the presidential debates this time around. It would be better if the light could also charge a radio."

Now she was on fire, waving her arms. Two other modifications to improve the lantern came in quick succession.

I watched David's face: he listened to each question and answered respectfully. And then, inspired by Teresia, he, too, told the truth, explaining in understandable terms what the company could try to change and what would be too expensive. She may not have liked every answer, but she respected his candor.

Though this simple scene should be the norm in business–customer interactions, two human beings considering each other's best interest—the level of mutual listening felt extraordinary to me. I'd become accustomed to witnessing people avoiding telling one another the truth. I'd seen too many low-income "beneficiaries" pander as privileged benefactors spoke with arrogant certainty.

This scene was different. The towering man and tiny woman from disparate worlds were not just listening, they were *seeing* each other. They were speaking as absolute equals. In the space between them, call it love or divinity, were the seeds of mutual respect, the opportunity for each of them to be transformed.

By listening, Sam and Ned discovered that once their customers made the first step from kerosene to solar, they quickly wanted more. D.light went on to design a suite of products, ranging from a simple five-dollar lamp for the poorest up to full home systems that included multiple lights, a cell phone charger, a radio, and, if they could afford it, a flat-screen television. As investors, we began to understand that there was an "energy ladder": once people got a taste of clean energy, they wanted more of it.

And why wouldn't they? Imagine living in utter darkness once the sun goes down in your home, regardless of where you live. Now visualize living in a rural area, lying on a mat on hard ground, hearing the sounds of animals and of howling winds, not knowing what creatures are crawling around or over you. Think of being a woman alone with her small children while her husband works far away to earn their daily bread; consider her fears that an intruder might be lurking outside her isolated hut, hidden in the night's blackness. Such troubles and terrors add layers of stress to the weightiness of poverty.

Then picture the dignity of flicking a switch and illuminating your room. For anyone who lives without electricity, the feeling can be miraculous. The scores of customers I have met over my years investing in d.light have reframed the way I understand the power of electricity. A radio can stave off loneliness and bring the outside world into a postage stamp–size room. A light can quell a dark night's fears and insecurities. A charged cell phone can connect you to love and protection.

We miss many opportunities by assuming we have the answers. Ned and Sam succeeded where many other endeavors did not because they approached the poor as co-creators in solving the problem of energy access. Through repeated listening, they helped their customers realize that they were there to serve them, not simply to take their money.

And because the d.light team listened, and did the hard work to follow up on what they'd heard, more than one hundred million people now have clean light and, increasingly, electricity. That is about one-third of the entire population of the United States.

Sam, Ned, and the d.light team also helped ignite a clean energy revolution that could change how Africa brings electricity to all its people, averting long-term climate change effects in the process. Imagine the human potential, the human *energy*, that might be unlocked by this solar-powered electricity.

Listening is a lifelong process. It requires continual practice, especially when we've become too accustomed to believing that our own assumptions are correct. I learned this truth for the umpteenth time on an incredibly hot day in Bahawalpur, Pakistan, an agricultural center in one of the country's most fertile areas, also known for its extremist madrasas. I'd gone there to meet a group of women weavers. They were sitting by their looms outside, beneath a thatched shelter. Their husbands were farmers who borrowed from our agricultural bank investee, so I knew the families were building savings.

At the time of my visit to Bahawalpur, d.light was selling a seven-dollar solar lantern with great success, especially in East Africa. I hoped to see d.light come to Pakistan, where the electricity grid reaches only about 65 percent of the nation's two hundred million people and, even then, might bring electricity for only two or three hours a day in some areas. I enthusiastically described the solar light to the women's group, marketing its attributes and asking if they'd be interested in buying one if we could bring it to their country.

Twenty pairs of tired eyes stared at me. No response.

I asked again. This time, a heavyset woman with a husky voice, a brown veil draped loosely over her hennaed hair, her face shining with sweat, leaned forward on ample haunches. "We don't need a light," she said flatly. "Bring us a fan."

For a moment, I was speechless and stared back. "A fan? I don't have a fan. I have a light."

"We don't want a light. We want a fan."

"But this is a great light. It will allow you to stay up later. Your children can study. You can work in the evenings."

She cut me off: "We work enough. We're hot. Bring us a fan."

Until that moment, I'd never considered the importance of a fan as opposed to a light. When it is so hot that even the cows lie down, a fan can matter more than a light. Plus, people already had light, even if it came from dangerous, smelly, expensive kerosene. In East Africa, where the nights are cool, people don't ask for fans. But customers are not the same in every market. Once again, I was reminded that if you want to serve, you must begin by listening, not assuming.

That night at my guesthouse, I took a cold shower and lay beneath the ceiling fan, grateful; never before did I so appreciate a fan.

Fast-forward a few years. Acumen began to invest in solar companies in Pakistan. I visited a family compound in the Punjab region that appeared unchanged since the sixteenth century: men in turbans, women in purdah, farmers using hand tools and plows in their endless fields of mustard and sunflowers. The family I spoke with had recently purchased a solar home system from a local company that included multiple lights, a cell phone charger, a radio . . . and a fan. The woman of the household told me that the fan impacted her children's ability to study more than the lights. "The fan keeps the air moving at night and the insects at bay. My children can sleep, which makes them better students." I nodded, remembering what I had learned during my visit to Bahawalpur.

We miss so much by assuming we have the answers. Instead, learn to listen with your whole body. Listen with your ears, your eyes, all your senses. Listen not to convince or to convert, but to change yourself, spark your moral imagination, soften your hardened edges, and open yourself to the world. When we fail to listen to those the world excludes, we lose the possibility of solving problems that matter most to all of us. But when we succeed at listening with all our attention and empathy, we have a chance to set others and ourselves free.

Chapter 5

YOU ARE THE OCEAN
IN A DROP

If deep listening enables seeing beyond another's words, understanding identity can provide potent tools to empower and unite. Identity can also be a trap, dividing us from one another, sometimes with toxic or even deadly consequences. Learning to navigate the many layers of your own identity, while also expanding your awareness of the multiple layers of others', is an essential twenty-first-century skill, one that can take a lifetime to acquire. Begin on the path to mastery by discovering the many stories that can be only yours.

I was born the eldest daughter in a patriotic American immigrant military family. My childhood memories are filled with identity-shaping moments: Catholic school and Mass on Sunday, elders telling me to "be a good girl" (and to earn good grades), and the constant rhythm of warm, boisterous family events that usually included polka music and folk dancing. Each school day, I pledged allegiance to the American flag; weekly, I made the Girl Scout pledge "to serve God and my country, to help people at all times, and to live by the Girl Scout law." That my dad did several tours in Vietnam reinforced the ideas of self-sacrifice and commitment at the core of my sense of self.

On Sundays, I would sit in church next to my mother, who always dressed up and sometimes covered her head with a black mantilla, her beautiful face serene. While at church, she did not reveal the spitfire woman so familiar to me the rest of the week. Priests and nuns encouraged us to give "to the hungry children in China," and though I was only five or six years old, I regularly dropped half my fifty-cent allowance in the poor box at the back of the church. An empathetic child, I grew increasingly aware of the disparities around me, though I still saw the world as divided between good guys and bad guys—and I assumed I was one of the good guys.

As I grew older, my life choices added contours to my sense of who I was, challenging what I had believed and my understanding of where I belonged. By my mid-twenties, my work experience in scores of countries across Asia, Africa, and Latin America made me yearn to know the world in its manifold layers. I wanted to belong to the world, too.

The more I encountered, the more I questioned and, unsurprisingly, the more I changed. With each change, I came closer to my true self. This required jettisoning beliefs and practices that no longer served my expanding understanding of the world or of the identities I was choosing to inhabit.

At the age of twenty-six, I sat down with my beloved father and told him that I was questioning whether I could continue to call myself a Catholic. I still remember the disappointed, confused look my questioning caused. I loved the stories and the Gospels, the rituals and music—in so many ways, I *was* religious—but I didn't love how the Church excluded; its actual practices too often countered my own beliefs. I could not reconcile that some people were welcomed into the

Church's community, and others were not; nor that women were so diminished within the Church's hierarchy.

I asked him, "I've worked alongside people in Muslim and Hindu and other religious communities and want to understand more about them. Aren't their 'essential truths' the same as ours?" And didn't true spirituality have to do with seeing yourself in every other human being, and they in you?

Life had been teaching me what sages and saints had written about for centuries. As the American poet Walt Whitman wrote in "Song of Myself" in 1855, "I am large. I contain multitudes," singing through his poetry to an expansive identity reminiscent of the words of the thirteenth-century Sufi poet Rumi: "You are not a drop in the ocean. You are the ocean in a drop."

By this time, I could no longer embrace the idea that my truths were of a higher or even separate order from those of people practicing other religions. I was grateful for my religious education but yearned to explore beyond its solid edges. I had begun to see myself as entangled with other peoples and other faiths, ideas I carried within myself: the ocean in a drop.

It devastated me to hurt my father. The conversation I had with him challenged me much more than when I informed my parents that I was leaving Wall Street to work in Africa. Our debate about religion threatened our family's core identity, potentially puncturing the heart of my most personal community. My heart ached, for I wanted no one's approval more than my father's and mother's.

"Will you ever go to church again?" my father asked, not with anger but with quietude.

"I will when I am home with you," I responded. I didn't want to renounce or fully abandon parts of what I'd been given, but I understood the need to embrace the new as well.

I promised that my deeds would make my parents proud. I hope to this day that they have.

As I went on to experience more people and places, the various parts of my identity became more nuanced. As the saying goes, you will never know the East Side till you move to the West. By working and living in other countries, I began to see America, the land of my birth, in more complex ways. I loved my country's ideals and felt grateful daily to be an American woman. We are a can-do nation of immigrants from all corners of the globe, exuberant in our sense of possibility, proud to be a place where anyone, regardless of birth status, can achieve greatness. Even today, when I run alongside the Hudson River, I silently salute Lady Liberty, gratefully acknowledging her welcoming promise to all peoples seeking to make their lives on her shores and to contribute to the American experiment.

Yet, just as with Catholicism, I also grew in awareness of the more shameful parts of my American identity, which continue to limit the nation's full potential. This includes the legacies of American imperialism suffered by Native Americans, the still-open wounds of slavery, and the unjust number of incarcerated young men of color. I began to recognize that every one of us, and every society as a whole, is a mix of light and shadow. In that realization, I found, and continue to find, extraordinary potential for growth, for relationships and self-discovery, for a new idealism grounded in the gritty, sometimes ugly realities of everyday work to be done.

Thirty years after that conversation with my father, I feel profoundly grateful for my multiple identities, both inherited and chosen. Each part of me is a chance to connect to others. Growing up in a big immigrant family made interacting with more community-oriented people in Africa, Asia, and Latin America feel closer to home for me. My Catholic upbringing helped me connect to other traditional religious communities, as I understood what it meant to prioritize family, daily rituals, and prayer, and to honor religious leaders who interpret holy texts. The daughter of an army colonel, I am comfortable considering myself a citizen soldier, and I respect the discipline, diversity, and leadership grown by the military. As a New Yorker, I feel a kinship to residents of big cities such as Mumbai and Karachi, Nairobi and Lagos. My inherited love of literature has connected me to new places by making conversations with strangers easier, providing a means of conveying curiosity rather than tired assumptions about their societies.

Each of us contains a multitude. The more identities we carry within, the more chances to discover that we are at once unique and bound by commonalities. So, as the Nigerian writer Chimamanda Ngozi Adichie asks, why, then, do we reduce individuals to a single story, a single identity that can too easily be infused with our greatest fears about one another?

I witnessed firsthand the fragility and potential deadliness of reductive identity during the aftermath of the Rwandan genocide. I sat in foul prisons listening to women whom I had considered friends rant about the evil of the Tutsis while fully believing the Tutsis would have murdered the country's other main tribe, the Hutus, had not the Hutus killed them first. Those encounters taught me that monsters and angels exist in every one of us.

Our monsters are the broken parts of ourselves, the shames and hurts and grievances often carried from generation to generation. If we do not confront them peacefully yet directly, those broken parts make us vulnerable to externalizing our pain through anger, violence, or a deadening bitterness. In times of insecurity, the divisive language and policies of demagogues prey upon our weaknesses, urging us to cast blame for our problems on those who are deemed "other." Too often, such language successfully entreats us to do horrendous things to one another.

I have lost too many friends to violence in the name of identity. Perhaps this is why I believe so strongly in the Lebanese French writer Amin Maalouf's explanation (in *In the Name of Identity*) of how identity operates within each of us. According to Maalouf, we each maintain a "hierarchy of identities" that rise and fall depending on whether a particular identity is threatened. When one of our identities is attacked, it becomes easy to perceive ourselves *only* as that identity, for how others see us can have a significant impact on how we see ourselves.

Think about your own diverse identities—your gender, religion, race, ethnicity, tribe, sexual identity, citizenship or refugee status, your schools. Which parts give you pride? Which parts shame? I'd be surprised if most didn't give you both. You might be a vegetarian or a carnivore; an extrovert or an introvert; an athlete; someone who loves classical music or hip-hop, novels or nonfiction; a nature lover or an urbanite—likely, your mix includes at least a few contradictions. Our personal commitments form aspects of our identities, too. Now think of those times when a single part of you felt threatened and you were reduced, either by others or yourself, to a single identity. The world plays along in these moments, flattening our sense of self to the point of caricature.

My own identity shape-shifts when confronted with the world around me. I feel more American when I am being questioned at a dinner party in Karachi about U.S. drone policy. When I am held at U.S. immigration for questioning because of all the Pakistan stamps in my passport, I become equally a global citizen and an American who wants my country to treat immigrants with greater respect. Perhaps, instead, we could start by understanding the many identities inside ourselves, avoid the temptation of labels and the demonization of others, and search for common ground in those who might seem different at first blush.

If holding our multiple identities and recognizing that *all people* carry myriad identities within themselves is a crucial step toward navigating difference in an interdependent world, a second essential skill is understanding how others perceive you, especially with regard to power and privilege. Throughout my twenties, I sharpened the first skill by interacting with other cultures. In my early thirties, a painful confrontation with the more privileged parts of my identity had to take place before I could fully learn the second skill.

In 1996, Peter Goldmark and Angela Blackwell, president and senior vice president, respectively, of the Rockefeller Foundation in New York, determined to build a leadership program to confront "the fault lines of race, class and ideology in America." Four years earlier, Los Angeles had exploded with riots over the acquittal of police officers who'd brutally beaten Rodney King, an African American motorist. The 1991 beating had been caught on video and seen hundreds of millions of times (before smartphones or Facebook). Because of the riots that followed the beating, more than 2,300 people were injured, 62 were killed, and the city experienced a loss of more than a billion dollars. Over the next four years, across the United States, identity politics grew more hostile.

The Rockefeller Foundation's most senior leadership wanted to try to do something about a deteriorating civic conversation in America. The two leaders of the foundation tapped me to create and lead this new program. I had already learned something about navigating differences while working in Rwanda, and I had tried to become a respectful listener as well. I loved the idea of confronting the fractures of American democracy through investing in diverse young leaders and was elated to build a program that would support their development. At the same time, I also felt that I was exactly the wrong person to lead that program. I was white. My orientation was more global than local. I had dreamed of investing in *businesses* that served the poor, not supporting individuals to lead.

However, the need was there, the opportunity was there, and no one else had stepped in to build something like it. My mentor John Gardner, whom you met in chapter 1, reminded me to be more interested than interesting. "You will learn to understand the rest of the world better if you do the work to know your own country," he said to me. "You'll be able to speak with greater humility if you can speak from experience about the challenges that your own country faces."

After much thought, I decided to start a new chapter in my life and let the work teach me. Together with a small, diverse and mighty team, I helped create the Next Generation Leaders program. The scope of our ambition thrilled me, though when we started, I had no idea of all that I'd have to learn to give the program even the slightest chance of success.

On the first evening of the NGL fellows gathering, as everyone sat down to dinner, I formally introduced myself. Twenty-four fellows sat around a horseshoe-shaped table, representing diverse slices of the American pie, including a Korean American leader of a community group from New York City, an African American leader fighting to eliminate the death penalty, a fighter pilot in the marines, and a gay Latina activist for immigrant rights, just to name a few. After welcoming these fellows, I began: "I hope we will use the group itself not only to explore differences but to understand one another, so that we in turn might better understand ourselves."

Heads nodded as I spoke. Though I was nervous, I thought, So far, so good.

Given our diversity, I continued, we also hoped to define rituals as a means of creating shared experiences and, thus, bonds among us. Each night, before dinners together, I suggested that a different fellow start the meal by sharing a poem, a blessing, a quote, or silence. Each fellow could choose whether to share his or her own tradition, whether religious or atheist, or to honor another one. What mattered was the fellow's gift of reflection and an openness from the rest of the group to receive it.

An African American minister from Chicago stood up that first evening, choosing traditional words of thanksgiving for the meal we were about to eat and ending with a quiet "Amen." Many in the group repeated the amen, but a young African American activist stood and accused me of "making this a Christian thing." I reiterated that we hoped to create the space not for what separated us but for what we shared. He fired back that people shouldn't be forced to hear dinnertime prayers. Heads nodded in agreement.

The evening had barely begun, and I'd lost the group.

Over the next few months, the group regularly devolved into arguments about identity rather than focusing on how we might actually solve problems. I hired two elderly white scholars to lead "Good Society" sessions, a powerful exercise taken from the Aspen Institute, in which participants reflect on their own values by interacting as a group with the writings of philosophers and activists spanning from Plato to Hobbes, Rousseau, King, and Mandela. Upset that the readings mostly came from "dead white men," some of the fellows refused to participate.

I did not know how to handle the situation, and the two facilitators ultimately left the session. The same young man who had raised issues around having a minister share a prayer made it clear from the beginning that I, a white woman of privilege, should not run a program built for a diverse collection of emerging American leaders.

Part of me thought he was right. My own insecurities stunted my ability to bring my whole self forward, though that was precisely what I was asking the group to do. Ultimately, the group avoided rigorous debates about how society might do better at encompassing our diversity. Opinions, not reason, dominated. Some fellows remained so busy defending their own identities that we collectively failed to make the effort to engage with the identities of others.

The lowest point of the year occurred at the end of a seminar, during a go-round in which each fellow shared an insight or question from the week's activities. When it was the African American activist's turn, he suggested that this was the right moment for me to resign. I thanked him for his comments, but I had no answers, not for the unasked questions swirling in the room and not even for the questions I'd posed myself.

The weight of the room's silence and the staring eyes of the fellows pressed in on my chest, intensifying my feelings of shame and guilt. Even though I'd put heart and soul into working with my team to create and fund this program, and had delivered on the promise of a group that reflected America's diversity, I had failed to facilitate difficult yet constructive conversations. For nearly an entire year, I had been unable to build a sense of wholeness and a connected group that could learn from itself. And rather than share the burden of failure with the group, I erred in thinking that the program's deficiencies were the sole responsibility of me and my team.

Later that night, after a good cry, I finally came to a reckoning with myself. The young activist had pinpointed one of the most unresolved parts of my identity: my privilege. It didn't matter how I perceived myself. What mattered in that moment was how *others* saw me. Until that experience, I saw myself as an industrious woman from a big, middle-class family who had paid her way through college and business school and who would face the monthly stress of school debt repayments for yet another decade. As a young person, I was aware that being a white American afforded me vastly better opportunities, but I also wanted to claim the "scrappy independent woman" part of my identity that was unafraid of sweat and hard work.

Yet, if I did not fully see myself as a woman of privilege, my identity had expanded to include working at the Rockefeller Foundation with a well-used passport and a Stanford MBA. If I hadn't been born an elite, I had certainly become one, regardless of how I saw myself. Only when I was able to integrate the person I had become with the person I once was would I be able to serve in ways that mattered.

Finally, I understood: by hiding parts of my identity, I had been denying myself and others what I could bring to the table. Because I had not laid the groundwork to know myself and claim a legitimacy for running the program, I had never been able to address the polarization that held the room hostage to identity politics and made it difficult for everyone to focus on the other issues at hand. I had failed to recognize that identity, our own and that of others, is always in the room.

Given all this, should I then resign? My resolve came slowly but clearly. No. Absolutely not. That young activist did not have the sole hold on what was right and fair. There were many in the group who told me privately, and repeatedly, that they were acquiring new insights and skills, and they urged me to stay the course. So, I would take this as an opportunity to grow personally and to expand my understanding of both the challenges and opportunities identity brings. I also realized in those days and weeks of reflection that we would succeed in building a cohort of diverse leaders who worked across lines of difference only if we selected people who were open to changing themselves. Without personal transformation, a moral revolution is impossible.

By the second year of the fellowship, I was able to lead with greater self-awareness and confidence. Rather than simply "checking," or distancing myself from, my privilege, I learned to know when and how to use that privilege of authority as an asset to create space so that other voices could be heard. I was more able to recognize, and call out, when a fellow, holding tightly to an ideological stance on either extreme of the political divide, was making constructive conversation impossible. When a fellow complained in that first year that the Rockefeller Foundation represented the imperialist capitalist elite, I simply stared, almost fearing to respond. But during the second year, I made it clear that everyone in the room, by virtue of choosing to join the fellowship, would have a new element to his or her identity. As fellows, they would have greater access and privilege that, in turn, required additional responsibilities.

I understood that my job was to make the conversation safe enough for all sides to feel deeply uncomfortable at times, and to grow from it. It was to challenge anyone who was throwing around easy assumptions, asking them instead to ground their perspectives in principles for which they stood. It was to remind myself and every one of the fellows that if *every one* of us was not open and willing to change ourselves, we would never be able to change the world.

My painful stumbles at the Rockefeller Foundation gave me a powerful new set of skills with which to navigate identity. First, know yourself. Second, be open to the multiple identities others might carry within themselves. Third, the person or organization with greater power in a particular moment must be the bridge that extends understanding to those with less power. Without this bridge, real conversations won't happen.

Keep in mind that privileges tend to fluctuate depending on context. Every one of us might feel powerful in certain situations and powerless in others, based on how we perceive ourselves and how others impose on us their ideas of who we are. The more you are aware of the power you maintain in each situation, the more likely you are to gain a truer understanding of others.

Though I could not have known it at the time, in pushing me way beyond my comfort zone, that painful year with the Rockefeller Foundation's leadership program broke me open and allowed me to stretch to find new parts of myself. I don't say this lightly; I realize that knowing all the parts of ourselves and being aware of how others see us is more of a struggle for some than for others, and it can be more challenging at various stages of our lives. Moreover, some people have single identities imposed on them in ways that can be life threatening. This is precisely why understanding identity—which is wholly different from learning to play identity politics—is such an important skill to learn and teach. We grow not in easy times but in difficult ones. In our moments of greatest division and fear, might we all become less comfortable and forge more nuanced understandings of our own identities, thereby opening ourselves up to explore the identities of others?

In 2015, I traveled to Bahawalpur, Pakistan, to discuss values and principles of moral leadership with a group of young Pakistani Acumen fellows who hailed from all parts of the country. Some young men wore jeans and polo shirts; others, traditional Pakistani *shalwar kameez*, long tunics with loosely fitted cotton trousers. Women, representing about 40 percent of the room, wore a mix of modern and traditional clothing as well. It was the first time I was meeting this particular group, but I felt a kinship given our shared global community.

After I asked which living people would qualify as moral leaders, I mused that the youngest Nobel Peace Prize winner in history, Malala Yousafzai, Pakistan's own daughter, was the Antigone of our times: courageous, noble, and powerful in her pursuit of justice.

Half the room agreed with me, some with a sense of national pride. Half shook their heads in disgust.

"She is a CIA agent," one young man said.

Another chimed in: "She's simply a tool of the West. The rich Americans love her because it fits within their story."

When I pushed to understand, the group began arguing with one another, their words flying past me. One of the members, a young bearded man, sat silently, scowling. I asked the group to quiet down, and I turned to him: "Why have you opted out of the conversation?"

"Malala is no hero of mine," he explained. "Her story has been manipulated to make the West feel good about itself."

People around the table jumped in, both to protest and to agree. I asked them to hold back and give the young man space to say more.

He continued: "I'm from Swat, just near Malala's village. We were one of the most progressive places in the country. We educated our daughters and sons in our valley. But after the 2004 earthquake, the Taliban came down from the mountains. They said Allah was punishing us for our evil ways and began to rule the area. Since then, we have lived with violence and fear in our midst. Schools were shut. Life became more difficult for us. Yet the world sees Malala and thinks we are barbarians who need to be saved by the West. It is not right. Those same people who love her and despise us don't want to acknowledge that the U.S. *created* the Taliban to fight the Russians in Afghanistan. And now the U.S. blames the Taliban for any of the violence to justify dropping drones on Northern Pakistan, on civilians. Why don't we ever hear about girls who escaped U.S. drone attacks? Why don't we ever make *them* heroes?"

He didn't stop there, but instead described wounds inflicted on his sense of identity from Pakistanis themselves. "Even those Pakistanis who say Malala is an angel," he said, "don't hide their surprise that she is so educated. They think our region is backward, that we are second-class citizens. It makes us feel more separate and, somehow, disgraced."

We could have paused, agreed to disagree, honored his reaction as one justified by his being part of a wounded community. But we would have lost the chance to dive into the layers of what Malala represents to so many in Pakistan. We would have lost the chance to collectively unpack the statement that "the West loves Malala and despises people from Pakistan's northern territories." Moreover, had we stopped, that young man may have been known from then on through the single story of being a Muslim from Swat. And he is so much more than that. He is a proud Pakistani; a lover of literature, of dancing, of sports; a university graduate. He is a father, a son, a brother, too. Also important, he's a teacher who runs a school for boys and girls in his home city, and he has gone to great lengths to protect girls' rights to education.

The conversation about Malala threatened his Pashtun identity. As Amin Maalouf would have predicted, in that moment, the Pashtun man spoke only from the part of himself that felt personally wounded—and thus, "Pashtun" was raised to the top of his "identity hierarchy," reducing his story to a single narrative. If we had not had time as a group to consider the complexities of this man's life experiences and the story of Malala herself, we could have become even more divided. Instead, we deliberately created space and time for uncomfortable conversations among people who, above all, valued listening and moral imagination.

You might be wondering what happened next, whether either side was convinced by the other. We never fully agreed as a group as to whether Malala was an angel or an agent. Yet most of the fellows admitted later that during that uncomfortable conversation, something within them individually, and in the group as a whole, shifted. At the very least, the larger group came to understand the hurt of Pashtuns in a more personal way. And at the end of our time together, one of the more privileged members of the cohort spoke about the shame he felt for remaining silent in the past when friends had insulted Pashtuns.

That unresolved conversation also elevated how we saw ourselves as a group. At the essence of the Malala exchange was the interplay of human dignity and identity; a yearning to be recognized and acknowledged; an unspoken promise: if you do not attempt to reduce me to a single identity, I will try to see you as a more integrated person as well. While we may not have fully resolved whether Malala was a hero, this was the resolution we needed: a commitment to acknowledge one another not just within the confines of the room but in the open spaces of the world.

The conversation about Malala prepared me for a surprising interaction I had in Dubai a few weeks later. I had been invited to speak to twenty professional women at a steel-and-glass restaurant atop one of the city's imposing skyscrapers. The scene could not have felt more different from our simple retreat in the agricultural fields of southern Pakistan. The middle-aged women were dressed traditionally in *abayas* (long, flowing black robes) and *hijabs* (head scarves), and obviously were very wealthy, exuding the confidence that comes from operating at the highest levels of political and professional achievement.

I spoke about my work and my hope to contribute to a new kind of philanthropy in the region. When I finished, the elder stateswoman of the group thanked me, then posed an unexpected question: "What do you think about Malala?" she asked. She clasped her hands and placed them gently on the table in front of her.

This time I was prepared. I started from a place of identity, acknowledging that while she was just a young woman, Malala had come to symbolize a tension between the West and the Muslim world, at least for some. I acknowledged that young women and men have been killed by the Taliban *and* by U.S. drones, and that with such violence, our children and the poor are the ones who lose most.

And then I shared my own belief that regardless of the circumstances that made Malala a teenage celebrity, she was using her privilege as a platform to stand for young people across the world, and doing so with respect for her religion, her parents, and her country. She may have been born a Pashtun girl from Swat, but now she belongs to all of us, and the world is better for it. I ended with another acknowledgment of my hosts: "I love this region and recognize the unholy partnership between fair-weather friends in both Pakistan and the United States. Both sides have dirty hands. It is our children who bear the brunt of violence and despair. It must be to us as women, as citizens, as mothers and sisters and aunts, to stand for building a peace that goes beyond politics, so that all children can grow to become what they deserve to be."

The elder woman smiled and said, "Yes." And then she was quiet for another moment. I wasn't sure what was coming next.

Finally, she said, "Thank you. Now we can talk."

Being aware of and acknowledging the identities others hold is a key skill for navigating complex conversations. Once that group of twenty professional women in the room had become even slightly more trusting, we could speak more freely of politics and philanthropy, of the situation of women in the Middle East, and of problems in international development.

Ultimately, our future as a human race depends on all of us subscribing to a revolution of morals in which we each commit ourselves to something beyond ourselves. We spend so much time focused on what we believe to be true rather than opening ourselves to the ways others perceive the world. A peaceful, sustainable planet demands that we celebrate our individual multiple identities while recognizing the one thing we have in common: we are all human beings. We are born equal by virtue of our precious, blessed, wild humanness—and that is enough to bind us to one another. Each of us is the ocean in a drop.

Our shared humanity is strong and vast enough to encompass our beautiful diversity. Think of yourself as a bridge extending forward so that others might walk across. Commit to stretching beyond your comfort zone to meet those whose realities are different from your own. You might be surprised at what you find on the other side.

Chapter 6

PRACTICE COURAGE

I was a child of the 1960s, a time of heaving change, when cracks surfaced in ancient institutions and the tightly woven fabric of society began to loosen. In fourth grade, girls were allowed to wear "nice pants" on Fridays to public schools, and even my Catholic elementary school stopped requiring uniforms. Through Vatican II, Pope John XXIII transformed the Catholic Church's relationship to the modern world. The birth control pill was introduced, and movements for civil rights and human freedoms broke out across the globe. Even then, most girls refrained from sports, took home economics in school to learn to cook and sew, and were taught to be polite at all times.

Luckily, my parents believed that their growing tribe of boys *and* girls could do anything. When I was nine, my father coached a middle school football team in Fort Leavenworth, Kansas. He brought me to practice one day, and some of the boys teased him: "Coach," they said, "you didn't tell us you had a *girl.*"

"Yup," he said, "but she's as tough as you are." He then

challenged two of the boys to a pull-up competition with me. I wanted to die of embarrassment—until I was actually in the competition; then I wanted to win. And, at least in my dad's memory, I did. My mortification gave way to a secret pride in being physically strong, a self-perception that became a superpower. In an age when most girls were cheering on the sidelines for boys playing sports, I wanted to be nowhere but on the field itself.

Necessity prompted my parents to instill a scrappy entrepreneurial courage in their brood. Raising seven kids on a military salary was no easy feat. When my brothers and I complained that "everyone else's moms" bought them Levi's jeans or Converse sneakers, our mother would give us the evil eye for wanting to be like everyone else. "You don't need to wear brand names," she'd say, disappointed. "You are *Novogratzes*. But if you seriously feel the need to be like other people, I'll make a deal with you. I'll cover the cost of plain jeans or sneakers at the Army Post Exchange, and you pay the difference for the branded ones."

My parents believed that each of us was capable of doing anything we set our minds to. And having someone play the role of encourager is one of the biggest gifts any of us can receive. It reinforces the courage that comes just by believing you count, that you're capable of something. (It doesn't really matter what that something is.)

As a result of my mother's deal making, we were always looking for entrepreneurial ways to earn income for greater independence and, sometimes, to buy those Levi's. I started babysitting when I was ten, then went on to work behind the ice-cream counter at a Howard Johnson's at fourteen before ultimately bartending while still in high school. And I made and sold Christmas ornaments door to door to earn enough money for school trips. Each experience required facing into discomfort—knocking at the houses of strangers to introduce myself, to ask people to buy things I'd put my heart into making. I had to learn to deal with rejection, to make decisions for myself and to handle money. And while the first or second or sometimes tenth time I tried something might still feel uncomfortable, each experience expanded my worldview, even the most incremental of victories imparting me with the belief that life could be a great adventure if you were willing to dare.

Courage is not the absence of fear. Courage is the ability to look fear in the face and continue to walk forward. All of us have something that frightens us, whether or not we admit it, and there are as many forms of courage as there are of fear. Only by nurturing our courage will we prevent our fears from making and then keeping us small.

Childhood gave me the courage to take physical and entrepreneurial risks, but it did not prepare me to speak truth to power. The institutions that grounded my youth did just the opposite, in fact, reinforcing the idea that girls especially were supposed to be "good" and respectful. Though I might have imagined myself a maverick, I also was groomed to be polite and considerate, without being honest or tough enough to ask for what I truly needed.

As a child, when I most needed courage to use my voice, I lacked any skill or sense of my own power whatsoever. After a long night of babysitting, a neighborhood father drove me home. He parked the car in our house's driveway, turned to me as if to say good night, and suddenly began kissing and forcing himself on me. I pleaded for him to stop, and fought to get out from under him, but I was also, somehow, polite until I managed to wriggle free.

I was twelve years old. I can still remember my outfit: a

pink gingham button-down shirt tucked into bell-bottom jeans with little houses embroidered around the waistband and an oversize pink comb in the back pocket, my long hair in braids tied with little white ribbons. I had never before kissed a boy nor really even considered the possibility.

I rushed into the house and saw my brave, loving father talking at the kitchen table with one of his best friends. The only word I could muster was *hello*. I scrambled up the golden shag-carpeted stairs to the bathroom and jumped in the shower wearing all my clothes. Sitting in the bathtub, the water pouring over me from overhead, I felt dirty and ashamed, confused and hurt. I never babysat for that family again, coming up with all sorts of excuses to avoid doing so.

For decades, I gave no external voice to my internal hurt, at least not to adults. I must have believed, or known, somehow that saying aloud what had happened would upset the social order of my world. I knew that my parents would have been devastated. My father was the kindest man I knew, and he had returned from Vietnam only months before. My mother was fierce, fearless, and focused when it came to raising her brood. I could not bear the thought of hurting either of them.

I dreaded the very notion that my father might injure the neighbor in his desire to avenge me. And what of the man's wife and children? I convinced myself that silence was a better option. I had neither permission nor practice to say aloud the true things that might need to be said, even if they harmed the reputation of a respected member of the community.

Forty years later, when I heard the news of the neighbor's death, I felt an unexpected sense of freedom. Now I understand that I was caught in a system that required the silence of the weak in order to protect and maintain the privilege of the strong. We remain voiceless because we fear rejection, shame, or letting others down. We stay silent when bad things happen to us or to those around us, afraid of losing status or love or the security of home. We want to keep our jobs or maintain the peace or, in some situations, stave off further violence.

Thankfully, systems that privilege some groups over others have begun to erode. A generation is more willing to confront ugly truths, openly recognizing that acts by some to denigrate or hurt others are unacceptable. People are finding others to stand in solidarity with them, even if they live in different communities. For any of us to be free, we must all be free.

Finding one's own voice and using it is one of the most difficult kinds of courage to develop. It grows from discovering and valuing our most authentic selves, regardless of the systems and structures that otherwise might attempt to define us. For those who've been injured, this requires courageously confronting our own trauma and injuries. But courage is a muscle. The more we exercise it, even in small ways, the more courageous we become.

Sometimes life gives us opportunities to do the right thing, even at a possible cost to ourselves. In my first job, I recognized a worrying pattern in a Swiss bank that had significant loans outstanding with Chase. It looked to me as if the bank would fail. The country director in Geneva ridiculed me as a baby banker who clearly had no understanding of the way Swiss banks operated. My boss discouraged me from politically ruffling powerful feathers. But I had triple-checked my work, and I knew that my job was to raise concerns, even if the worst-case scenario never happened.

And so, I did. After an anxious, wakeful night, I sat at a big wooden desk across from the bank's towering, powerful country head. My knuckles were white from gripping the seat beneath me, and I felt as if I were in a roiling storm at sea. My voice quaking, and resisting the urge to vomit, I relayed my conclusions to the disdainful country leader. Later, I submitted my report to the global credit committee. I didn't sleep for the next two nights, anxious that my findings might result in the loss of my job.

A few days later, the bank failed. My reputation was burnished, and I internalized the importance of speaking my truth, even through trembling lips. I also tried to remind myself that things could have gone differently. The bank might have stayed afloat, and my boss could have seen me as a troublemaker. But at least my integrity, even if known only by me, would have remained intact.

That experience fueled my courage to stand up for my beliefs when I switched from banking on Wall Street to microfinance in Rwanda. A local priest had accused our microfinance organization, Duterimbere, of usury (charging illegally high interest), though we charged women just 12 percent a year to borrow versus the informal moneylenders, who charged as much as 10 percent *per day*. Knowing I'd survived my initial discomfort at Chase, I was more prepared to confront the cultural guardians in Rwanda. In Rwanda, the stakes were higher, for they were about not just my career but our organization's very mandate.

Even after I was gaining the courage of my convictions and learning to fight for my beliefs, I still lacked confidence in another area of my life: public speaking. When it came to speaking in front of groups, it took me longer to learn that fear is conquerable if you confront it, understand what lies beneath it, and then face it, often repeatedly, until you make it a friend. As with most hard things, that takes practice.

The particular fear of public speaking showed up early in my life and persisted. When I was a teenager, my knees would knock whenever I had to make a presentation. On Wall Street, we had to study public speaking as part of our training. After witnessing my nervous laughter and rapid-fire speech, my instructor told me that I was perhaps the worst public speaker she'd ever encountered. That single comment set back my confidence even further. But I knew that public speaking would be an essential skill for leading change, so I looked for opportunities to present to small groups, sometimes staying up half the night to practice. If a speech went well, I'd gain a bit of confidence. If it was a flop, I'd think about what I could learn from the experience. It took years to get to the point where I sometimes even enjoyed public speaking.

During this process, I also learned to calm my nerves. As a young woman, I'd listened to the advice of those who told me to "pump myself up" before speaking. That only stressed me further. "Imagine the audience naked," someone else suggested. But that image distressed me. Pretending I was a superhero served to keep the attention on myself, and didn't work, either.

It took years to realize that I had it all backward. Rather than focus on myself, I needed to direct my attention to the audience. I was speaking, after all, as a messenger, not a protagonist. My job was simply to be an instrument of love, I'd remind myself, whether to inspire thought or provoke action. Rather than attempting to stare down my ego, I would try to allow my ego to dissolve. This approach turned out to be a grounding mechanism, enabling me to get out of my own way and do what I had come to do.

All of us are at times strong and at other times fragile, certain and unsure—these contradictions are part of the human condition. Sometimes, the same people who display nerves of steel when negotiating high-stakes deals find it almost impossible to provide difficult feedback to beloved employees. Each act requires its own kind of courage, and few of us are fearless in every situation. Some people fear being viewed as imperfect or unworthy; instead of courageously communicating mistakes or failures, they hide small problems, denying partners or friends or investors the chance to help rectify the situation. Sometimes those same problems grow into full-blown disasters, making manifest the very fears the person tried to avoid.

At Acumen, we've lost important investments because a team member lacked the confidence to advocate for a risky deal, assuming others would think him crazy for proposing it. But if you want to play it safe, you shouldn't get into the business of change. Change involves risk, and risk, which is not the same as recklessness, requires courage.

Institutions can try to make it easier for people to take risks, but it is up to each of us to practice small acts of courage so that we build muscles to do the right thing. Regularly, we should ask ourselves, what is the cost of not daring? Of not trying? Of not speaking up when it matters?

Practice courage until you become courageous. Think of fear not as a bad thing, but simply as a mechanism to alert you to emotional or physical danger. The more you confront what lies beneath the fear, the more you can tackle it through repeated confrontations and small victories. Those wins, ultimately, will prepare you for the times when the world needs you to stand bravely in the fire and take on the seemingly impossible.

And even then, for some, there are times (hopefully rare) when the stakes of change suddenly rise to a matter of life or death, when you have only fraught options and you find your-self flying without a net. In such situations, what separates those who are able to master their fears from those who run or hide is *purpose*.

One leader with this gritty, muscular courage, one fueled by a singular purpose and commitment to community, is Andrew Otieno. A mild-mannered man of slender build, Andrew worked as a senior leader at Jamii Bora Bank, a Nairobi-based nonprofit microfinance organization imbued with an ethos of self-help and mutual support. In addition to serving as a senior leader of Jamii Bora, Andrew also founded and ran a health clinic close to where he was born in Kibera, the largest urban slum in Africa.

Life threw many challenges at Andrew, giving rise to a steely toughness to backstop his temperate demeanor. But even he could not have imagined the gut-wrenching fortitude he'd have to muster after Kenya's 2007 presidential election caused an eruption of tribally driven violence that left Andrew's cherished community raging with riots and fires.

Andrew oversaw Jamii Bora's office in Kibera. The lending operation served tens of thousands, including the more than 1,700 merchants who operated out of the fabled Toi Market, one of East Africa's largest open-air bazaars. Known for selling secondhand clothing and just about everything else, Toi was a vibrant, colorful, glorious mosaic of tiny kiosks that enabled millions of dollars to flow through the marketplace, supporting the livelihoods of nearly a hundred thousand people each year. It was there, on the edge of the market, that Andrew's office sat, witness to an artery of economic growth and opportunity. For some, that market provided the best route out of poverty.

One night, during the raging post-election weeks of rioting, a couple hundred young men looted and razed the market in a massive brawl that left many wounded and several dead. In the morning, all that was left on the hallowed ground of Toi were ashes and charred stumps that indicated where market stalls had once stood. The community was not only trauma-tized, but left with no place to work, and most were at risk of falling deeper into poverty. Toi could easily have become a war zone.

The young men's night of destruction had been fueled by wounds of identity and a desire for vengeance. With their riot-ing, the men—mostly unemployed, and many of them gang members—had aimed to "reclaim" land they believed was rightfully theirs. Kibera had been established as a land grant to Nubian soldiers who'd fought on behalf of the British Army in World War I—albeit without a formal title to show this. Over time, other tribes migrated to Nairobi, and Kibera, its popula-tion exceeding two hundred thousand, was declared an infor-mal settlement in which all land belonged to the government. Presumably, many of these young men were descendants of the Nubian soldiers and thus wanted "their" land back.

Yet, without Toi Market, the community as a whole lost its primary economic artery, its lifeline to commerce, and its connection to the larger city. Merchants had lost their wares, which for most accounted for nearly everything they owned. Some residents had lost family members. All of them lost some sense of security, for there was no one visible to protect them.

Andrew Otieno could have only one purpose at this point: rebuild the market.

How to do that, though, in the face of the young vandals who had terrorized the community? Since the post-election violence, the international NGOs and even the police had stayed away. And the community had been left on its own.

But Andrew understood that he was not fully alone. The founder of Jamii Bora, an irrepressible Swedish woman named Ingrid Monro, had spent decades committed to building an organization in which people helped and accompanied each other. Because she had immersed herself in the Kibera community, Ingrid also understood the life-or-death importance of the marketplace. She recognized that while Andrew and other local leaders had to lead the rebuilding of Toi Market, she had a form of social capital to offer them: connections to international agencies. While Ingrid traveled to Europe to raise money to rebuild Toi Market, Andrew remained in Kibera to navigate at the local level.

In early 2008, soon after the worst of the riots, I met Andrew in Jamii Bora's bright offices in a more central part of Nairobi to discuss a different matter related to Acumen's investment in the organization. The calm and beauty of the city stood in stark juxtaposition to what I'd heard about the ugly violence and danger in the slums just a few miles away. Andrew and I spoke about the Toi Market situation and how so many people in Nairobi were going about their business as if nothing had happened to their neighbors.

"For many," Andrew said, "Kibera is both in our own city and a different world altogether."

He asked me to go with him to see the market. No, I said. I didn't want to show up as a voyeur, and I knew there were enormous security risks. But Andrew would not hear of it. "No outsiders will go and witness," he said, "so no one understands the situation. We are left on our own. If Mama Ingrid fails to find the money, you might need to help us, too."

The fires were still burning in Kibera when we arrived, and reports of continuing violence jangled my already tense nerves, though I found comfort in Andrew's calm and sober grace. The Jamii Bora lending office, situated at the market's edge, had been ransacked. There was not a single desk or chair or computer in sight. Still, a long line of women sat on the floor, hoping they might borrow again, or at least speak to someone.

Andrew and I, along with his colleague Gabriel Kadidi, ventured into the empty marketplace, past young men hammering stakes into the ground to mark their territory. A number of merchants shuffled around their old work spots. A man folded newly washed baby clothes on a tiny bench that he carried in and placed in the spot he'd rented when there was still a market. "Who do you think will risk the danger to come here to buy baby clothes?" I asked, needlessly reminding him that violence was still widespread.

He sighed. "Probably no one. But I've no food for my family and nothing left but hope."

As if on cue, a man in a tan jacket ran over to Andrew to tell him that, on the other side of the market, a few hundred feet from where we stood, a muscular young man in a dark blue T-shirt and jeans had struck an older man's bald head with a machete. The man in the tan jacket and another resident then carried the wounded elder to a beat-up car parked by Jamii Bora's office. In the chaos, I never learned what happened to the perpetrator, but the injured man survived. There were no police in sight.

I couldn't help but juxtapose the scene with the perfectly folded baby clothes piled amid the burning embers of the marketplace. I desperately wanted to flee.

"How will you get this market built in light of the danger, these tensions?" I asked Andrew. "Who will help you do it?"

I could understand Andrew's urgency, but I could not see how he would pull off the reconstruction—not soon anyway, and not without more violence.

"We will find a way," Andrew whispered, his face strained. I hated to leave him. I was returning to a place that provided me every opportunity and liberties I too often took for granted—freedom from fear, freedom from abject poverty, freedom to travel. Here in Kibera, despite the destruction and even the deaths, despite the burned-out storefronts, razed marketplace, and marauding young men, ordinary citizens would still get up, get dressed, and go to work. They would find a way to bring their children to schools taught by heroes—more ordinary citizens doing extraordinary things. This experience with Andrew renewed my commitment to become braver myself, to show up more fully, to be more compassionate.

A few months later, I was back in Kibera. Astonishingly, so was the market. Ingrid had raised the money, and Andrew had overseen a peace process that would rival the Oslo Accords in bringing sworn enemies into cooperation and agreement. I asked him to walk me through how he'd managed to erect a thing of beauty from a heap of ashes and rage.

"It wasn't easy, but I took one step at a time," he said. First, he'd searched the refugee camps and discovered the leaders of the looting: a local gang member and his sidekick, let me call them David and Jonah. Andrew explained his plans to rebuild the market and restore peace, and he told the men he hoped for their blessing. The men shouted that they wanted revenge, not peace. Their intention was to build two hundred houses where the market stood, one for each member of the gang. Waving a machete, Jonah threatened to kill Andrew if he didn't comply. Andrew didn't move. He recognized the men's grievances and restated his goal to rebuild the peace—and that he needed their help.

I'd meet David later that day. He was handsome, with dark skin, high cheekbones, cool black eyes, and a steely expression. His hair was cut close to his head, and his muscular arms were as solid as granite. If Jonah could threaten with his weapon, David's eyes made it clear to me that he'd killed people before.

Andrew had neither the tools of a trusted judicial system nor the funds to offer reparations. The currents of identity tore differing truths through the tortured landscape, and Andrew could see only imperfect options each way he turned. He understood from the start that without security, he'd have to find a solution to peace that included the young vandals. The thought sickened him: rather than punishment, these men were being rewarded for the destruction they'd wreaked. But the trade-off for that injustice was a functioning marketplace that served thousands.

A few days after the failed first meeting with David and Jonah, Andrew had returned to the refugee camps. David and Jonah still thought he was nuts, but David decided they might as well listen to this man who was willing to be as crazy as they were, just in a different way.

By that time, the residents at the camps were starving. The UN agencies were slow in distributing foodstuffs, and the market was not functioning. Jamii Bora had been given the job of distributing food to residents in the camps, but Andrew knew the food itself was vulnerable to looting now that the market was gone. He also understood that those most likely to create trouble were the same young men who had razed the market in the first place. So, he made the risky, albeit strategic, decision to hire David and his guys, both ensuring that residents could access needed food and taking a step toward building goodwill with the young men. As he said to me, "No outsiders were securing the peace. I had few options, so I chose one with the greatest chance of meeting the community's most urgent needs."

In time, Andrew, stressing the potential gains each would

make, negotiated a deal in which all sides would contend with some loss. He aimed for solutions grounded in realities of the community itself that positively touched the broadest swath of people. He hired the gang members to rebuild the market, and then negotiated with the market residents to allocate two hundred stalls to the gang, one for each of its members. The utmost he could achieve was imperfect, and the imperfect would claim almost everything Andrew could muster within himself.

The young men didn't quite get houses, but they now each owned a business and a chance to rebuild their lives. To the market residents, Andrew offered an uneasy peace and the chance to get back to work, to stand again on their own two feet.

"Look, if you help these boys, we will have the market running again," he said. "If you don't, there will be trouble, because the boys believe this is their rightful territory. And there is nowhere else for them to go." To me, Andrew acknowledged that he had struggled mightily to find a way to arbitrate between competing truths. What made that arbitration possible was focusing on his goal and communicating as often as he could—with everyone.

With no good options, Andrew found the courage to make a compromised decision, acknowledging it was the best he could do. His effectiveness at bringing the community along with him was a master class in leadership. While many organizations temporarily left Kibera after the violence, Andrew committed personally to keeping Jamii Bora operational. He showed up daily to his empty office at the edge of the market in case problems or disagreements arose, aware that while the short-term fix was a new marketplace, healing the tensions and wounds beneath could take much longer.

Andrew survived unimaginable pressures. He risked his

reputation and his life for his community. And he himself seemed surprised by his bravery, which was ignited and sustained by an abiding commitment to his people, his place, his nation. We cannot choose what happens to us, but we can choose how we respond. In courageously confronting ugly realities, and by knowing not only what he stood for but for whom he stood, Andrew collaborated with other brave men and women. Together, they prevailed in rebuilding a market and restoring peace.

Andrew's challenges were extreme, but they are not unique. Leaders all over the world must contend with situations in which they must "navigate the gray" or look unflinchingly at ugly truths and make a decision anyway. The only way to survive and thrive is to acknowledge the imperfections, to say aloud that you could not be trying harder, and sometimes, to compare your outcomes to what would have been had you done nothing at all.

All this takes courage, and gaining courage requires practicing it.

The same night that the young man lifted his machete and struck an innocent elder in the Toi Market, I flew to Switzerland. The next morning, surrounded by happy, wealthy children bundled in warm winter coats against a backdrop of fluffy snow, I suddenly experienced a sense of vertigo. Images of the violence I had experienced over many years rushed through me: a farmer holding the barrel of a shotgun against my throat on a lonely road in Mexico; three men in Tanzania attacking me on a beach; a random guy waiting at a bus stop in Guatemala City pointing his gun at me. My brain was in overdrive. I thought of the man who inexplicably punched me in the gut as I walked down Fifth Avenue early in the morning on Valentine's Day, and the man in Malaysia, physically smaller than me, whom I think I hurt more than he hurt me. I was always a fighter in the moment, but these incidents were rising up to haunt me.

I wept for my younger self, for the friends I'd known who'd been wounded or murdered for their beliefs or for merely being in the wrong place. I wept for the images of the bodies of people slain in Rwandan churches and the layer upon layer of violence that is part of human society.

Since that night, there have been other moments when an image, whether in the newspaper or on the streets, summoned these painful memories, bringing back the taste and smell of fear. The fears would arise like Harpies, screaming. It took years for me to recognize that I would defeat those demons not by using the fallback skills of my early identity (courageously confronting the "enemy" and shaking off the pain or, more truthfully, running away from it), but by accepting my own vulnerability and self-doubt. It was only when I began to love the imperfect and broken parts inside of me that I could show up with my whole self. I'm still working on it.

I finally understand today what I wish I had known long ago: If we see ourselves only as victims, we risk failing to recognize our own fallibility, and this makes it impossible to accept the flaws of others. If we see ourselves or others only as perpetrators, we extinguish possibilities of redemption. If we refuse to see at all, we trap our diminished selves in darkness, relinquishing hopes for growth and renewal. In all such cases, we thwart our potential for wholeness.

The neighbor who attacked me as a twelve-year-old girl may have been told he was worthless his entire life. I'll never know. The man with the machete in Toi Market may have internalized a sense of irrelevance and invisibility, making it easier for him to cast blame for his hurts on another tribe than to take personal responsibility for them—just as it is easier for the wealthy people in his larger community to blame him alone rather than acknowledge the structural impediments to this young man's flourishing as well. The cycle of violence, internal and external, individual and structural, can be endless.

Unless we have the courage to stop it.

No one escapes life without broken parts. When we find the courage to repair what is broken inside ourselves, to reconcile the hurts we've internalized and the hurts we've inflicted on others, we can finally renew our fragile world. We can finally comprehend that our individual and collective wholeness is necessarily enmeshed. This kind of repair requires *moral* courage, the will to face fears and to fight for those who are unlike us, especially those outside our own families or tribes.

So, practice courage. It will prepare you for those times when you, and the world, need it most.

Chapter 7

HOLD OPPOSING VALUES
IN TENSION

"I would be happy to give you money if you promised you'd build five *million* houses, but five *hundred*?" The wealthy venture capitalist spoke with an almost comic level of disbelief. "Can't you be a little more audacious?"

It was 2004, and I had traveled to Palo Alto, California, to an office on Sand Hill Road, the storied "Main Street" of Silicon Valley. I sat in a large glass room across from a man with a mien of certainty and the insistent mannerisms of someone for whom time is definitely money. The venture capitalist had made a gazillion dollars betting big in fast-paced technology start-ups, a few of which had created billionaires, at least on paper, seemingly overnight. The irony that I was there to pitch the idea of "patient capital" to this person was not lost on me.

"Patient capital," I said, "is an approach to early-stage investment in entrepreneurs who are stepping in where markets and government have failed the poor. Acumen's patient capital approach is straightforward, but new." I went on to explain that we raise philanthropic donations and invest for ten years (or more) in companies that serve the poor. We bring management support, introduce new markets and networks, and make a long-term commitment to partnering in order to impact the lives of the poor. Patient capital focuses not simply on maximizing profits but also on holding the tension of both social impact and financial returns.

The VC did not conceal his allergic reaction to the idea of trade-offs. "If you build a highly profitable business that people value, it will grow virally," he said, using a popular (if overused and misunderstood) Valley term.

"Yes," I said, "but we can't assume that we'll build a profitable model in the short term. Reaching people with limited income and hobbled trust requires a balance that harvests the strengths of both markets *and* philanthropy. Finding that balance doesn't happen overnight."

I started to explain that we had just invested in a new development community outside Lahore, Pakistan, that aimed to construct five hundred houses. Building a development for slum dwellers on land so barren it resembled a moonscape would require not just infrastructure such as water and electricity, but also creating Pakistan's first-ever mortgage product for low-income people that was sharia-compliant (governed by Islamic religious law).

The VC stopped me again. "But five *hundred* houses? That's not very interesting."

"It will take time to build trust among low-income people who have had scam artists sell them houses on paper and then disappear," I said. As in most developing countries, Pakistan's urban poor tend to live in large, informal slum settlements on the outskirts of town, with little or no government infrastructure. It took time to navigate the bureaucracy and corruption endemic to low-income housing everywhere. And the product had to be priced so that people who paid forty or fifty dollars per month in rent could afford to buy a house.

I could hear myself growing defensive. Something in the VC's manner made me feel rushed and inarticulate. I was, clearly, failing to persuade him.

"I still don't understand why you're thinking so small," the VC repeated. "This is the problem with social enterprise: you work at the margins without really changing anything." He said he might be interested in five *million* houses. "But five *hundred* houses?" he repeated. "Why even bother?"

Now it was my turn to be frustrated. Hadn't the VC heard the challenges I'd just described? By then, I'd spent more than twenty years trying to make change in low-income communities, and understood the complex ground realities that made solving poverty so challenging. When you are investing in a technology platform company such as Google or Amazon, yes, you can reach millions of people seemingly overnight. But housing for the poor? If it were that easy, there wouldn't be a seven-million-housing-unit shortfall in Pakistan. (Today, the number is closer to ten million.)

"Why even *bother*?" I responded. "Because if you don't bother, we're stuck with the status quo. And that isn't working for the people who most need change." I repeated the reasons we needed to be both patient and urgent. "We *will* be audacious," I said, "as soon as we have a model that can grow to scale. Creating that model requires innovating in unknown territory."

The VC was unconvinced; he passed on the opportunity.

My conundrum was one common to anyone introducing a new approach to solving old problems. While I could paint a vivid picture with lived experiences of what had *not* worked in international development, I had no proof of how the patient capital model *did* work. I could only describe what *could be*.

And there was little my team and I could do about that except to continue to seek and support innovations that might succeed, and accompany them until they did.

I left the meeting feeling diminished by my failure to convince the VC of the merit of the patient capital model and daunted at the thought that it might take years before the model was taken seriously.

It was even more confounding for me to see investors who had rejected a patient capital model turn around and give millions in philanthropy to splashy top-down ventures with little chance of long-term success. In the early 2000s, a number of well-intentioned entrepreneurs-cum-donors made grand proclamations about building thousands of schools, adopting communities, or fashioning merry-go-rounds as creative ways to pump water. These were big bets on scaling solutions, with audacious promises of massive short-term payoffs. Missing from the equation was the humility to start by listening to what the poor actually needed and wanted, to focus on building a business model that actually worked, and only then, to focus on growing the solution to reach millions.

After a few years of enormous spending, many of the projects failed, leaving empty schools, broken wells, and more disenfranchised and mistrustful communities. The philanthropists moved on—some having learned from the experience, some blaming the communities rather than examining their own choices. Solving complex problems is rarely accomplished with a silver bullet or a single approach. Effective leaders looking to bring about change have no choice but to hold opposing values without rejecting either.

The venture capitalist was right in that we must have the audacity to imagine a different future. John F. Kennedy's audacious vision for landing on the moon inspired a nation to do the impossible. We must have the kind of audacity that drove a new generation to build technologies that changed the way humans interacted across the globe. And we must balance that audacity with a new humility that considers and is accountable for the unintended consequences of our actions.

If audacity and humility must be balanced to shift systems, so must accountability and generosity. Our current institutions have traditionally leaned toward one or the other rather than encompassing both. We assume the business sector is more accountable and efficient; the charitable sector, more generous. Because Acumen bridges both the nonprofit and for-profit sectors, co-investors have phoned me more than once to demand that Acumen make a grant to help an ailing company we were both supporting. One memorable call came from an irate co-investor in Africa who reached me on a Saturday morning at my home in New York City. He was unhappy with my team's insistence that all co-investors work with the troubled company on the same financial terms. The investor believed that Acumen alone should bail out the company, which was navigating treacherous financial waters.

"Why us alone?" I asked. "Why wouldn't you also support the company?"

"You are patient capital," he responded. "You can afford to help."

I almost laughed out loud, for he represented a much larger and richer institution, one that could presumably take much more financial risk than Acumen.

"We can be generous, yes," I said, "but equally, we focus on accountability. If you are interested in the future of the company, we'll work through how best to do it *together*—and take equal risk in doing so."

My response triggered a powerful reaction. "You get on

stages and talk about love," this investor said, "but when it comes down to it, you're just like everyone else."

I was taken aback. "I'm sorry, but our focus is *patient* capital. It is not stupid capital," I said, deliberately using language that I thought would resonate with him. I believe in love, to be sure. But real love requires setting expectations and helping people gain the capacities to meet those expectations. That entails being willing to have uncomfortable conversations, to know when and how to step in financially, and to understand when a bailout creates dependency. Real love is not a soft skill. In this particular case, we needed to send a message to the ailing company, and the market, that all investors believed in the company and were working together to turn around its operations—head and heart.

Those who see the role of business as solely to make a profit often employ either-or thinking. But presupposing that profits alone signal the existence of social good limits our ability to think creatively, collaboratively, and constructively, not to mention realistically. The mirror image, relying solely on charity or government, is limiting as well. In a world of interdependence, we will flourish only if we move to "both-and" thinking, integrating purpose and profit, generosity and accountability, the community and the individual.

Holding on to both-and thinking requires sustained effort. It is much easier to focus on profit alone or to ignore financial discipline and throw money where your heartstrings tug you. But if you are looking for easy solutions, you probably will not realize substantive change.

In 1527, the Italian philosopher Niccolò Machiavelli wrote about the tensions between leading with love or fear, two proxies for generosity and accountability. While Machiavelli's Prince preferred fear, young leaders often tell me that they would rather lead with love. But if fear or accountability on its own can be punitive and diminishing, love or generosity alone can create dependency and entitlement. With both, progress hangs in the balance.

As the world becomes more entangled and institutions more diverse, the capacity to hold opposing values without rejecting either has emerged as a critical skill for solution building. Consider a simple mantra: "Use feelings of discomfort as a proxy for progress." The disquiet may not make decisions easier, but it will help you identify the forces you are dealing with, buttressed by both conscience and reason.

Jawad Aslam, the young man who created the five-hundred-unit housing development I describe at the beginning of this chapter, perfected the art of holding opposing values. It took him many years, but learning to allow for and acknowledge dual perspectives, he was able to build homes, not just houses, for a community that had always scraped by on the margins.

I met Jawad in Lahore in 2006, about a year after he'd arrived. A Pakistani American from Baltimore, he'd had a solid career in commercial real estate until the events of 9/11 roused in him a yearning for more. He experienced firsthand the mistrust that many Americans began to harbor about Muslims and felt his own religious identity deepen. The time seemed right to travel to his parents' homeland to try to be of use.

Once in Pakistan, Jawad apprenticed with Tasneem Siddiqui, one of the nation's gurus of affordable housing, who offered him the chance to lead a project called Saiban. In order to sustain itself, the Saiban housing development needed to be profitable. From the beginning, Jawad was more interested in building community than merely constructing physical pieces of property. All people would be welcome as potential home-owners, provided they were there to live and actively participate in the community. Unlike many developers of affordable housing, he felt responsible for basic services, a sense of security, and an enabling of social cohesion. In turn, he asked residents to help tend the parks and common spaces, thus forging a sense of community while also empowering individual households to gain choice and freedom.

The nexus of these contradictory forces was the community mosque. People of all faiths were welcome to live in Saiban—and they came, not only from the slums of Lahore, but some from as far away as Karachi, a fifteen-hour drive. The home buyers represented most sects of Islam, with a small number of Hindu and Christian families (in Pakistan, Hindus and Christians each represent about 2 percent of the population). Each sect wanted to use the mosque for prayers on a daily basis.

But as there was only one mosque, giving every sect exactly what it wanted was infeasible. In Jawad's mind, there was no better way to reinforce the idea of a shared community than to ask all Muslims to pray together—and that would require some loss of individual autonomy, an independence each sect had enjoyed prior to moving into this new place.

At first, Jawad's view that the mosque could and should be shared isolated him: few agreed with him. In modern Pakistan, it is unusual to see mosques filled with Muslim worshippers of different sects; a Christian corollary would be Catholics and various branches of Protestants attending the same Sunday service. But Jawad conceived his seemingly radical idea as a chance to renew values of community within the context of modern diversity.

Moreover, there was precedent in Pakistan for sharing a mosque. Until the early 1970s, diverse members of a community would gather together in the local mosque each week to pray, whether they were Deobandi or Barelvi, both Sunni sects, or even members of a Shi'a sect.

Rather than capitulate to the modern tendency to want only what is good for ourselves, Jawad insistently argued for what was best for *everyone*. He carried this idea of the commons in tension with his commitment to encouraging each family to build their own house in whatever style suited them. While the residents appreciated the freedom to reflect their individuality in the homes they built, many residents disliked the idea that they would have to share the most sacred time of each day with people whose traditions diverged, however slightly, from their own.

Month after month, Jawad negotiated, cajoled, and arbitrated among the competing sects. "There were times when we had to stop meetings altogether because people became physical," he remembers. Residents wanted to feel comfortable and safe "with their own." Still, he never lost sight of his fundamental objective: a peaceful, diverse community that would ultimately reinforce a sense of belonging.

Finally, after more than a year, Jawad and the elders came to an agreement. The community elected a highly respected imam, who led daily prayers as all sects sat and prayed together.

My husband, Chris, and I were planning to visit Jawad at the housing development in May 2010 on what turned out to be the day after terrorists attacked two mosques in Lahore, murdering nearly one hundred people during Friday prayer. The tragedy was a cruel reminder of how hatred and fear of the other can lead humans to engage in abhorrent, murderous acts. Stunned and saddened, we decided to stick with our plan, almost as an antidote to the shocking violence the city had just witnessed.

As we made the twenty-five-minute drive from downtown

Lahore to Saiban, Chris and I sat in tense silence. Any unspoken anxiety vanished, however, as we arrived and walked
across familiar parks filled with laughing children, their parents relaxing beneath tall trees I'd seen planted years before
as tiny saplings. A big-armed woman sold candy and trinkets
out of her tiny shop to chattering neighbors. For a moment,
we forgot the violence just a few miles away; this tiny pocket
of the world was tranquil, comforting.

Chris remarked that the community also was more vibrant
than some suburban neighborhoods he knew in the United
States, where households appeared distant and isolated from
one another. I recalled the hardships Jawad endured in the
beginning of Saiban's existence, as he tried to convince residents to take responsibility for maintaining their collective
green spaces. He had planted those trees, hoping neighbors
would join him; at the time, they merely thanked him for his
efforts but offered no support themselves. He tried shaming
people. That didn't work, either. But as more houses were
built, a friendly competition naturally arose among various
blocks as each tried to make their park the best. The result,
finally, was a beautiful semi-urban oasis.

We approached a group of elders, all men, sitting outside
the mosque conversing with one another. They told us of their
pride in the community, how it had become a place of hope
for residents. Their children attend good schools, they said.
Jobs had come, too, and buses regularly transported workers
to town. As for the mosque, all was good, the elders said. One
of the men mentioned that during the recent spate of sectarian
violence across Lahore, their community was one where the
peace was never broken.

I reminded Jawad of the extraordinary number of grueling,
uncomfortable hours he personally had invested in listening

to individual needs and balancing them with his vision for a robust community.

He smiled. "Everyone here is a migrant from the city," he said. "Some come from as far away as Karachi because they've heard this is a welcoming place." He continued: "Nobody migrates by choice. There's always some hardship or reason why people have to leave the place they originally called home. Our job is to try to facilitate that process for them. And they in return have to learn to live with others who are different, which leads to some kind of loss for them, too." In short, Jawad had deliberately built a community, not just a development of individual houses.

Finding and maintaining the right balance between the individual and the community, freedom and belonging, competition and collaboration, requires moral leadership precisely because that balance can be discovered only by inviting constructive conflict for the betterment of the whole. Done correctly, efforts like Jawad's can serve as a model for new social infrastructure with the potential to bring out the best in people, asking each of us to manage the inevitable inherent tensions required to live in a community where all are valued.

If we ignore the tensions within ourselves, our organizations, and our societies—if we keep the conflicts internalized and unmentioned—they don't disappear. Instead, as soon as we begin navigating complex issues and decisions across lines of difference, those conflicts become exacerbated. The key is to recognize and give voice to the tensions in ways that both sides of a debate can hear, a sometimes thankless task, to be sure, yet fundamental to the practice of moral leadership.

In the winter of 2017, a group of about twenty Acumen fellows from India and Pakistan organized a series of video discussions among themselves. Most of these fellows hadn't previously met; and indeed, some had never had a direct conversation with any person on "the other side" of the national lines dividing India from Pakistan. But tensions between the two countries had been rising, and the two groups were eager to practice transcending the boundaries that separated them.

The groups of fellows from both countries created ground rules and reminded themselves to seek some truth in what the others were saying. They dared to utter the prejudices they held about one another. Mostly, they listened. The conversations were brave and tender; and sometimes, excruciatingly stressful.

I had the privilege of checking in with each group afterward, and I remember a Pakistani woman sharing almost apologetically how nationalistic she felt at times during the video encounters. "Suddenly, I became purely Pakistani and experienced moments of mistrust that gave me shame afterward," she confessed. This led to an important conversation about identity, and the ways in which it can impede our abilities to reach out to understand another's perspective.

While visiting Mumbai a few months after the video sessions, I spoke to a group of Indian Acumen fellows. The conversation was again grounded in identity, but what happened next was a powerful example of the challenges of holding tensions when belief systems push us to retreat to comfortable corners. One young man said he'd felt proud of participating in the conversations, reaching across cultural and political differences in troubled times, so he posted a screenshot of the video call on Facebook.

"Almost immediately," he said, "I was deluged with hatred. What hurt most was that some of the most outraged responses came from childhood friends."

At home that evening, he shared his experiences with his parents, hoping for empathy. Instead, he met a dark wall of rage.

"It was bad enough that you decided to become a social entrepreneur," his father scolded. "Now you are consorting with the enemy. Your uncle died in the Partition. We have family in the Indian Army.

"You must decide whether you are with your family or with the enemy," his father continued. "You must decide if you are a true Indian."

The young man looked at me ruefully, and asked, "Is it possible to be both an Indian patriot and a global citizen?"

Hearing those words was heartbreaking, though I shouldn't have been surprised. The early twenty-first century has witnessed growing strains that reinforce in-groups that find strength in creating mistrusted out-groups.

I said to him, "If you define patriotism as being the best at the expense of other peoples and nations, and if you blame others for your own problems or refuse to engage, then you cannot be a patriot *and* a global citizen."

He stared as I spoke.

"But," I continued, "if you are willing to model a sense of belonging that translates into responsibility for the national good, and if you believe in celebrating the remarkable parts of your nation with the rest of the world, while recognizing exceptional aspects of other nations, then you are indeed a patriot. And the world needs more of such patriots."

Just as any solid relationship or familial unit needs to include strong individuals to thrive, so a family of nations requires healthy countries to work toward their own wholeness and contribute to the global community. Today's problems (climate change, inequality, refugees, outbreaks of disease and terrorism) know no national boundaries. We will solve them only if we can hold the uncomfortable tension of national priorities on the one hand and the urgency of our global challenges on the other. We must commit to building sustainable neighborhoods, companies, and nations, each of them locally rooted and globally connected, each giving more to the world than it takes.

Can I be a patriot and a global citizen?

Absolutely. Proudly. Even if sometimes uncomfortably.

In every country, we hear similar conversations. Our fears can propel us into corners where we hold ourselves hostage to ideologies that reinforce differences. We stop listening to the other side, fearing loss to ourselves, even if we don't fully understand what that loss might be.

In the United States, for instance, fear of immigrants and refugees has driven neighbors into two angry camps. "Build a wall!" one side screams. "Open borders," the other side retorts with equal rage. The actual details of either position don't seem to matter as long as each side feels satisfied with its own righteousness.

By allowing polarities to dominate a debate, we free ourselves from facing the painful trade-offs and costs that *every* choice entails. And we deny ourselves the opportunity to rediscover that we are better than we think we are.

We will not have any hope of finding humane, effective solutions until we quiet ourselves enough to hold the truths that, though seemingly opposite, do exist on either side. What if we slowed down enough to reach out and identify a truth or even a half-truth in what the other was saying? Both sides, one hopes, would acknowledge that there are no easy solutions to immigration in a world besieged by poverty, inequality, and climate change; a world in which the populations in rich countries are shrinking while the number of people in poor countries is growing. The population of the African continent alone is expected to double by 2050 and nearly quadruple by 2100. Only by daring to recognize the uneasy truths that lie far, far apart will we gain the chance to solve our common problems.

Rumi wrote, "Out beyond ideas of wrongdoing and right-doing there is a field. I'll meet you there." Eight hundred years later, we have a chance to breathe new meaning into this ancient wisdom. A modern moral revolution demands that all of us hold contradictions, even stark ones, within ourselves as well as between ourselves and others. For each of us, the first step is to reach across the wall of either-or and acknowledge the truths that exist in opposing perspectives.

When engaging someone whose views are opposed to your own, consider taking these three steps. First, seek, with eager curiosity, the truths in the other side's argument. Second, take a figurative stride, even a small one, toward the other, acknowledging where there might be common ground. And third, hold tightly to the *essence* of your whole self, while embracing other aspects of your identity lightly. You must be open to change and learning if you expect the other side to be the same. Whether we're talking to an impatient venture capitalist or tiptoeing through a political minefield, these skills can help us find better ways forward that may not please everyone but will bring more of us along.

After repaying Acumen for the loan to Saiban, Jawad Aslam went on to create a for-profit housing development based on a similar model. Nearly a decade after he first arrived in Paki-stan, he successfully sold half that housing company, providing Acumen and other investors with double-digit returns. He also raised twenty-five million dollars from a strategic partner who had deeper experience in housing than we did to build sustain-able communities across all of Pakistan.

And still, Jawad balanced opposing values in the way he shared success. Rather than keep the 50 percent of shares from the sale of the company for himself, he split them up among its employees, including the young man who serves the tea. Jawad has proven that mortgages can be made affordable to the poor—and sustainable to lenders.

As I write this, I cannot help but think of that long-ago conversation with the Silicon Valley VC. I wonder what that venture capitalist would have made of Jawad's accomplishments today. In addition to building eight hundred homes, he has built a model for affordable, sustainable community development from which countless others can learn. He helped housing policy in Pakistan become more transparent and accessible. In short, he lives a life capable of inspiring other change-makers across the world.

Though Jawad repaid our investment in his company with a healthy financial return, our partnership with him is forever: he is now on Acumen's Global Advisory, helping us navigate new challenges. Even if things had turned out differently and his entire housing development had failed, by holding firmly to his mission, embracing the tensions, and finding the courage to stand apart and do what was right, Jawad would have built something valuable: his character.

When we dare to understand the other, we find the seeds of our best selves.

I can't help but think of the housing crisis facing San Francisco. In that city, so close to where the VC and I had our long-ago conversation, some of the most successful companies in the world must confront the unintended consequences of the economic boom they've created: widespread homelessness, a by-product of inequality. How valuable would Jawad's learning, experience, and character be to that city today? Here, again, solutions will require both audacity *and* humility.

In every family, organization, community, and nation, there

are fields in which we all must dare to meet. A moral revolution demands that all of us do more to reach across the wall of either-or and to acknowledge the truths that exist at the opposite poles. Most of our solutions lie in the truths or partial truths on each side, "out beyond ideas of wrongdoing and rightdoing."

Chapter 8

AVOID THE
CONFORMITY TRAP

A few months before the financial crisis of 2008, a prominent Swiss banker invited me to serve on an advisory council for a new fund he was developing. The fund would invest in microfinance institutions that, in turn, would make small loans (from thirty to a few thousand dollars) to poor women in the developing world. "This fund is going to generate the highest financial returns in our portfolio," the eager professional said, "and there is little risk associated with it."

I felt a knot in the pit of my stomach. "So, you're asking me to join an advisory in which a Swiss bank plans to earn their highest returns from the poorest women in the world, at little risk to the rich? Doesn't that sound odd to you?"

The banker quickly responded, "Don't think of it as making money off the poor."

"How should I think of it, then?" I asked, "especially given your pitch that this fund will generate the highest financial returns *of all the funds you manage*."

The banker became a bit sheepish. "Fair enough," he said. "But don't you agree that a fund investing in microfinance banks is a step in the right direction? This will bring more money into a sector that needs to grow. This is a chance to do well by doing good." He added, "It would be great to have a voice like yours interacting with a bank like ours."

His flattery pricked a slight feeling of mistrust. "Traditional investors with no background in low-income markets looking for high returns make me nervous," I said.

"But you will meet wealthy investors on the advisory and build a relationship with our bank, which could help your own fund-raising," the banker responded.

I paused to work out what was bothering me. The Swiss banker seemed genuinely thrilled that his fund was creating a positive impact. But at the same time, he'd structured a conventional financial vehicle in a system that rewards greed without considering whether or how that system would deliver on its promises to "do good" for the poor. My feelings were complex. I was, and am, a believer in the strategic imperative of providing low-income people access to affordable credit to enable them to enhance their capabilities and choices. And we at Acumen had invested our own patient capital to help build several microfinance institutions when we believed our investment would be most catalytic.

Then it dawned on me. The key difference between the Swiss banker's approach and that of Acumen lay in how we each perceived means and ends. The banker saw financial returns as his end. If the poor were served—well, that was an ancillary benefit. He had never visited the microfinance banks in which his funds had invested; he'd never met any of their low-income borrowers. My mistrust was not of him as a person but of a system that would make decisions based on short-term profitability, not on whether those he professed to serve were seeing positive changes in their lives.

Distance easily dulls our moral imagination. In the banker's case, just believing that he could sell a product that allowed investors to "do well by doing good" was enough. He had geographical distance from those who would be making and taking out the loans, and that afforded him emotional distance, too. What mattered to the banker was generating high returns for his shareholders. What mattered to me was something else. I wanted to use the tools of the market as a *means* to solve poverty, not as an end. We were playing in different arenas, with different intentions. I thanked the man for his kind offer, but passed on the opportunity to join his board.

When a product for the very poor is marketed as doing good while generating outsized profits at zero risk for the very rich, a moral question is born. In a world of extreme inequality, what kind of economic system is just? By conforming to a system structured solely to maximize shareholder returns, we avoid taking personal responsibility for the answer to that moral question.

Conformity to traditional market priorities is a trap that can make it exceedingly difficult to do what is right. Decisions that depend on moral choice, not transactional effectiveness, are rarely straightforward once you are clear about what's at stake. If I had decided to join the banker's board in order to influence the fund's ongoing activities, yes, I probably would have met influential people who could have helped Acumen. But I ultimately needed to know that I would be partnering with someone who was at least open to going against the grain of shareholder capitalism.

A few months later, when the financial crash occurred, the economic system got a reckoning—and most everyone was touched by it. In the United States, many on Wall Street and on Main Street alike lost fortunes. Millions lost their homes.

Most traders agreed that the financial system had gotten out of control. Still, they defended their actions, arguing that they never did anything illegal, unable or unwilling to wrestle publicly with whether what they did was right. Meanwhile, millions of people with no financial cushion, caught up in the promises of "easy money," had risked their futures and paid a dreadful price. In the end, everyone lost. As for that Swiss banker, he never got his microfinance investment fund off the ground.

No matter how determined we are to do the right thing, we all fall prey to conformity traps within the system we've chosen. We want to "win," to appear successful, respected, or powerful, so we cut corners and tell little white lies. We hold our itching tongues when people around us demean those from another group—not because we are bad people but because we don't want colleagues or friends, religious leaders or classmates, parents or siblings, to think we are weak, disloyal, naïve, unsophisticated, or foolish. And sometimes, in the longer term, we end up causing harm; we end up becoming the person we said we'd never be.

Our anxieties germinate in the systems we inhabit. Who are we measuring ourselves against? Whose opinions matter to us? What does winning even look like?

Mustering the moral courage needed to do what's right, not what's easy, requires knowing when conformity is a force for good and when it instead muffles our conscience. The theologian Reinhold Niebuhr wrote that "groups are more immoral than individuals." By shifting the blame to systems bigger than us, we tend to convince ourselves that we have no choice but to "go along to get along." But if you dare to act on dreams of change, you must find the guts to stand apart while also building the relationships needed to design better systems.

The warning signs of traps nearby read almost like a bad poem:

> It's just business as usual.
> Everybody's doing it.
> And I don't want to look stupid.
> If I don't do it, someone else will.
> No one *else* is saying anything.
> Don't the ends justify the means?
> I really don't have another choice.
> I wouldn't do this just for myself.
> People are counting on me.
> Besides, I'll do it just this once . . .

Self-justifying phrases, uttered by you or those around you, separate you from accountability. Like the banker who was emotionally removed from the people his fund would have impacted, it's easy to insulate ourselves from our actions. But we *can* make the choice to be guided by our own moral compass and play for the long term. Stay close to people who keep you honest and who will stand by when you feel isolated, or worse. Keep in mind that business as usual remains that way until we change our definition of what is "normal."

It's also easy to be a critic who regularly finds fault rather than proposes solutions or, better yet, risks her reputation attempting them. So, avoid the trap of perfection, not just the trap of conformity. If you are a builder, there will undoubtedly be times when you have no choice but to compromise in service of a greater goal. Think of the gray areas Andrew Otieno had to navigate to reconstruct the market in Kibera. Moral leadership requires the judgment to make the right short-term compromises so as to realize the long-term change we seek.

Rejecting conformity outright is required for change. Until 1865, slavery was business as usual in the United States. The abolition of legal slavery began with those few courageous individuals who dared to go against the moral conventions of the time, conventions endorsed, in many cases, by teachers, parents, religious leaders, and, again, the law itself. Many who protested paid the ultimate price for their actions, and the abolition movement required strong allies to stand with them before the tide turned.

If you are a change agent, then you are by definition a non-conformist. You stand for something. Get used to the awkward-ness of turning right when everyone else turns left, and pursue what you know to be true. And before you partner or invest, do your homework to understand a person's character rather than be swayed solely by charisma or connections. I have been burned more than once by trusting someone because they had received ringing endorsements from people I admired.

In the same year as the financial crisis, Acumen invested in a company led by a magnetic, capable entrepreneur. (I've withheld the name of the company and country to protect innocent people.) At first, the entrepreneur gained significant momentum, and local recognition, for his highly efficient and profitable company. Our team was swayed to invest partially due to the entrepreneur's commitment to allocating a percent-age of the start-up's services to the poor. But the first time I met with him, *after* we'd invested, I was left with a nagging feeling that something was wrong.

Sometimes your gut recognizes what your brain initially misses. Within eighteen months of our investing, the company was thriving financially and creating significant impact. At the same time, our local team discovered that the entrepreneur was keeping two separate sets of financial books—one for us and a much-less-profitable one for the tax collector. When we brought this to the entrepreneur's attention, he explained matter-of-factly that "everyone does it."

Acumen has a strict ethics statement that every investor signs. The practice of keeping two sets of books is illegal and unethical. What, we asked ourselves, should our next move be? Here, too, we risked falling into the conformity trap. We assumed that if we took the case to court, we would fail. And when we reached out to a few investors to ask how they handled such issues, more than a few suggested that the practice of using two sets of books was, indeed, "business as usual."

We knew what we had to do, but it is not easy to write down profitable investments, especially ones demonstrating social impact. Writing off our investment would result in a hefty financial loss to Acumen. Yet, if we did nothing, we'd reinforce unethical behavior, reduce our legitimacy as champions for impact (even if only in our eyes), and take a painful hit to our own integrity. "Everyone does it" cannot be society's or any organization's standard for decision making. But doing the right thing can be soul crushing and frustratingly lonely when peers or colleagues would rather you "won" according to the rules of the status quo.

Our team at Acumen conferred: Were we willing to write off our investment completely if we couldn't find someone to buy our stake? Were we willing to go to court, given an unreliable justice system? And what if we could convince the entrepreneur to change his ways? Were we willing to extend our trust to him again?

We reached out to the entrepreneur to give him a second chance. He refused, reiterating that keeping two sets of books was accepted business practice in his country. I realized that our real failure had been in doing too little to understand this misalignment of values *before* we invested.

Corruption is a disease with epidemiological patterns that spread and fester. The poor suffer costly and sometimes harrowing permanent consequences: health services and police protection are sometimes denied unless bribes are paid, and those unable to pay, often innocent people, lose their health, their freedom, their livelihoods, and even their lives. Systems grow so corrupt that people feel incapacitated *unless* they participate in the brokenness of it all, and the potential of everyone to live with dignity is diminished.

The Acumen team decided to exit the company. We sold our shares at a relatively small loss to another impact investor that didn't mind investing in a company that was compromised and preferred to focus on its potential impact. For a year after the sale, we watched the company grow in its reach and prosper financially, gaining media coverage for its impact. Some, I'm sure, wondered whether, in this case, the ends *did* justify the means.

Some months later, I picked up a local newspaper and saw the face of the entrepreneur looking straight out at me. He'd been arrested for corruption. I hated to think of the people who'd lose basic services, yet I was relieved that we at Acumen had found a way to extract ourselves before the investment devolved into crisis. I was reminded again of why we invest in *character*, in those people willing to stand apart from the crowd, sometimes opening themselves up to looking foolish but always willing to grapple with doing the right thing for their customers, employees, and society, not just for the sake of profits.

Would the story still be persuasive if the entrepreneur had been wildly successful? I think it would. Acumen had to establish a norm, a code that our team and our companies would live by. In creating more just, inclusive, and sustainable systems, the means, not solely the ends, matter. You make change when you model change.

Even when you are proven "right," it is counterproductive to revel in righteousness. Even as we at Acumen breathed a sigh of relief that we'd exited the deal, I knew that luck had also played a role. I'm certain that we've made other mistakes in assessing character, and I have never met a single person without flaws, starting with myself. The best we can do is aspire to live with integrity, to tell the truth and expect the truth from those with whom we partner. Flaunting the moral high ground when others fall does little to compel them or us to do the hard work of self-assessment with honesty and humility. Your greatest calling card is your reputation for integrity. Treat it like gold, though it is worth even more.

A few years ago, one of the Acumen fellows cheated on his expenses. Like Acumen's entrepreneurs, our fellows sign statements of ethics, which make clear our expectations for their conduct when they join the Acumen community. Those statements reinforce an ethos that we are striving to uphold qualities of moral leadership. The *community* creates a support system for mutual accountability.

My senior team at Acumen was split on what to do. Some believed the fellow should be expelled from the program immediately. Yet he was deeply remorseful and asked for the opportunity to redeem himself. His boss reinforced his otherwise stellar performance and character.

After thinking long and hard about the situation, consulting both the fellow and two people close to the situation, my senior team agreed on giving him a second chance. We asked the fellow to write a letter to his boss and to me, sharing lessons learned. He also wrote a letter to his cohort of fellows, and a few weeks later, his in-person apology led to a powerful conversation about the community's norms and expectations. Everyone grew from the experience, and to this day, the young man has continued to excel not just in what he does but in who he is.

While every situation is different, one thing remains clear. As the American civil rights advocate Bryan Stevenson has said, "Each of us is more than the worst thing we've ever done." Stevenson explained this idea: "I think if somebody tells a lie, they're not just a liar. I think if somebody takes something that doesn't belong to them, they're not just a thief." If we banish someone from the community before considering all the circumstances, if we let go of a basically good person who has a fierce desire to grow and contribute, look how much we miss.

Our modern instant-feedback society offers ample opportunities to shame and blame, sometimes with destructive and even deadly consequences. Say a young person is caught cheating on an exam or stealing from her organization's petty cash. Perhaps, she felt great pressure to send money home to her parents. Maybe she was testing the system, or just being thoughtless. Although this is the first time she's violated the group's ethical contract, when a peer discovers what she has done, he posts a statement of outrage, publicly shaming the young woman in question. Within an hour, a barrage of angry voices rises in a pile-on of shock and humiliation. Notions of restoration or redemption, essential aspects of healthy communities, may quickly feel futile.

The scene is uncomfortable and all too familiar. Can we instead pause, try to understand, and focus on solutions? Might we all take a few moments of reflection before we comment on social media, thinking about what our words will mean to the person in question and the whole community?

* * *

In the early years after the Rwandan genocide, everyone in the country possessed the powerful and necessary right to accuse others of war crimes. That freedom also empowered some to use "I accuse you" for nefarious purposes, charging innocent neighbors because of past grievances having nothing to do with genocidal actions. Others made accusations purely out of greed. On a visit to the country in 1997, three years after the genocide, I remember the almost unimaginable anxiety and despair expressed privately by people who had been unjustly accused of horrible acts. Even a baseless accusation could tarnish a reputation by planting seeds of doubt in a society already plagued by mistrust.

While the circumstances are usually less dramatic, the internet enables all of us to be instant judges, which in some cases unleashes roaring mobs. Our online lives bring us close to those who think and feel like us. This is wonderful in many ways, but it also creates conformity traps. If we're not careful, we can get swept along in toxic forms of groupthink and mob behavior. We thus have a corollary responsibility to balance judgment with judiciousness, a responsibility requiring self-imposed discipline. Thankfully, the world is full of role models carving paths to what is right for all of us.

On March 15, 2019, a white supremacist attacked two mosques in Christchurch, New Zealand, killing fifty people in the middle of their Friday prayers. Refusing to conform to tired conventions such as speaking compassionately to the victims, sending thoughts and prayers, and blasting the murderer's name across global media platforms, New Zealand's thirty-eight-year-old prime minister, Jacinda Ardern, quickly called for changes to the system. She refused to use the name of the terrorist and moved within days to change outdated gun laws. With compassion and toughness, heart and head, the prime minister led with all her humanity, bringing out the best not only in her own citizens but in people across the world.

Constrained by neither female nor male stereotypes, Jacinda Arden acted swiftly to protect her nation's people and stood with moral courage for those who had suffered most. Her nonconformity set her apart in ways that invited others to participate. Taking the prime minister's lead, tens of thousands of New Zealanders gathered to honor their Muslim neighbors. Women of all ethnicities turned up wearing headscarves, as their prime minister did. Even the global media respected Ardern's leadership, refusing to splash the name of the terrorist across the world, thus denying him his twisted lust for infamy. Rather than simply mirroring those who had gone before her, the prime minister set a new standard for a powerful moral response to hatred.

Each of us has opportunities to avoid conformity traps and offer the world the best version of ourselves, whether we are a prime minister, a teenager, or a corporate leader. Fifteen-year-old Greta Thunberg of Sweden started a youth movement in 2018, waging a one-girl protest to fight climate change that eventually gained the attention of the entire world. America's most effective advocates for gun reform include teenage survivors of a mass shooting in 2018 that killed seventeen students at Marjory Stoneman Douglas High School, in Parkland, Florida. Young people are raising their voices and calling for change, and the world is taking note.

Brave CEOs, too, are standing apart. Bob Collymore, the beloved Kenyan CEO of Safaricom, made public his net worth and challenged his peers to do the same, though few followed his lead. He fought corruption relentlessly and modeled an ethos of service continuously. What made him a true nonconformist, however, was the way he lived the minutes of his life. Some of his closest friends grew up and worked in Nairobi's slums. During a time of heightened terrorism, Collymore fasted for Ramadan to demonstrate solidarity with Muslims.

"Never be ashamed of who you are," he would tell young people. "Never let people decide how you should feel about yourself. A person's a person no matter how small."

Bob died too young, at sixty-three, but because he dared to be his own man, his influence will last for generations.

We often start out wanting to be like others until an external event or situation forces us to confront the toll society's strictures impose on those who are different. Gayatri Jolly, a privileged young Indian woman, grew up assuming she would join her family's successful home care business as one of its first women directors. She attended the "right" schools in the United States and studied business to prepare herself. But back home in New Delhi, Gayatri found herself spending two years sitting in her family office feeling ineffective and, too often, ignored. Everyone, including employees, assumed she would work for her family only until she found a suitable husband. Instead, Gayatri told her father that the arrangement wasn't working. And then, with his support, she moved to New York City to study at the influential Parsons School of Design.

While at Parsons, Gayatri decided to build a company that designed and manufactured beautiful clothing, a company led, run, and aimed at women. Her social enterprise, which she called MasterG, would also train women to become *masterjis*, or expert pattern makers, a profession that in South Asia was held only by men at the time. Well-intentioned friends and relatives urged her to aspire to be a designer with her own collection, a much more conventional, status-oriented route. For Gayatri, the price of nonconformity was hearing others

make light of her desire to "help the poor" as if she were simply a "failed designer" on a mission.

Though aware of her privileged position in society, Gayatri
knew what it felt like to be invisible in her own family's business, and thus a sort of outsider. Time would teach her to
use her sense of invisibility as a gift. Coupling that with her
empathy for underprivileged and underserved women who
had none of her access, she was able to imagine using her privilege as a bridge to them. She followed a thread, an instinct—
that she had the skills and knowledge to offer the garment
industry—and in doing so, served a group that had for too
long been invisible.

In early 2017, I visited Gayatri's training center on the edge
of a semi-urban hamlet called Gwal Pahari, on the outskirts of
New Delhi. The village, home to the traditional Gujjar community, is a place with high reported levels of child marriage
and domestic abuse. Female feticide is also common. Indeed,
some of the young women in Gayatri's program suffer chronic
illness from repeated illegal abortions, forced on them by families who did not want to welcome additional daughters. Yet a
growing number of young women either escaped their families or found ways to secure their blessing to join Gayatri's
MasterG training program.

The tailoring room, a place usually associated with poor
working conditions, was bright and filled with young women
in their late teens and twenties, all of them moving through
different stages of pattern making and stitching classes. Some
sat at sewing machines; others learned to make patterns.
Gayatri had taken her lessons from Parsons and extended
them to these women.

Beyond practical skills, the program teaches the women to
think more freely, to create and give voice to their knowledge.

Asked regularly for their opinions and their decisions, often for the first time in their lives, these women necessarily confront the socialization that required them to be seen but not heard, to be nice and know nothing, and to believe that they were worth less than a man.

"Our community must break the pattern of prejudice against women," Gayatri says frequently, her pun intended to communicate action both to the women she serves and to the industry she hopes to reform. "To change the system, our women must begin by changing themselves." Gayatri dreams that some of the trainees will become celebrated outside the studio and serve as role models for young women across India and the world.

One of the *masterjis*, a petite young woman named Rajni Mourya, was slight of build with long hair and wide brown eyes and was attired in a bright pink-and-white dress with flouncy sleeves. Rajni's father, an informal laborer, had died when she was a teen, leaving her with a sick and debilitated mother and younger siblings to support. Upon her father's death, she dropped out of university to scratch out a meager income by providing tailoring services in her local area.

"Girls like Rajni weren't meant to succeed," Gayatri told me. Life changed radically once Rajni joined the MasterG Fashion Design and Skill Development Program. Seeing how Rajni cut patterns and tailored garments for her class assignments, Gayatri perceived a rare talent, and I soon saw what she meant. Rajni is now working full-time with Gayatri, pattern making and stitching for the company's upscale clients across the world. She is also pursuing a degree via distance learning.

Rajni stood at Gayatri's side to welcome me to MasterG. Rajni was learning English, so Gayatri did most of the talking.

"We're going to make a jacket as our gift for you," she said, beaming, adding that Rajni would be the one to take my measurements and do all the tailoring and finishing. Gayatri pointed to a small room where Rajni and I and a couple of the young women who could help translate would gather. While Rajni was expertly taking my measurements, I asked her what her dreams were.

"I want to be a Somebody," she said, adopting language commonly used at Acumen. I smiled.

As she was taking the last measurement, it was Rajni's turn to smile. When I asked her the reason behind her ear-to-ear grin, she blushed. "I got your measurements perfectly," she said. "I don't need to change anything."

"Anything of what?" I asked, not fully understanding what she was talking about. Her friend explained that she and Gayatri had already blocked out the pattern earlier, and Rajni was fairly certain of my measurements.

"But we've never met," I said, stating the obvious. "How were you able to guess my measurements with such precision?"

She seemed puzzled by my surprise. "Oh, madam, I watched you on YouTube," she said matter-of-factly. "That's how I could guess. I know your colors, too," she added. A few minutes later, she showed me an array of silks, each dyed a different jewel tone, all perfectly curated for me.

A generation ago, Rajni would likely have lived a life trapped by tradition and poverty, with limited freedom and little ability to support her family financially. Now she has access to a world-class education, a support system, and a steady income. She has a chance to dream in ways not afforded to most young women in her community, nor in any previous generation. Like Gayatri, she dared to be a nonconformist and, as Gayatri regularly says, "break the pattern."

Of course, Rajni and the other young women sometimes have to switch their mannerisms, behaviors, and even the way they speak when they are at home in order to survive in their communities. They still regularly face situations in which they pretend to know less than they do as a survival mechanism. Some hide their work and, most definitely, their dreams from family members. But more of them are moving out of bad marriages, setting up shops of their own, finding their voices, and building strength in the unity they offer one another. Already, the MasterG women are becoming role models for a new generation: Gayatri has trained more than a thousand of them, all of whom were tired of waiting for someone else to give them freedom.

Gayatri sees technology purely as a tool. She attracts customers based on her unique talents and then uses online communications to connect customers across the world to expert pattern makers like Rajni. In this way, she extends her privilege, her *social* capital, to bridge two worlds. Her pattern makers gain skills, self-confidence, and increased income. Customers are able to see the direct impact of their choices. If we learn to control it and not be controlled by it, technology does not have to divide us. It can be used to feed and strengthen relationships.

As for Gayatri, I have no doubt that she will be a famous designer. But her success will be a shared success. As Rajni and the other young women learn to trust themselves and fly, they will buoy Gayatri as well, enabling her to break ever more patterns. Instead of striving to gain a seat at the proverbial "table," she is building a table of her own.

The difference between Gayatri and that Swiss banker is that Gayatri avoided conformity traps. They both wanted to do good for the world. The banker, however, believed his job was to protect the short-term interests of his shareholders by valuing profit above all else, even though when markets turned, the most vulnerable stakeholders lost most. In contrast, Gayatri devised in MasterG an inclusive business model that refuses to see the world as separated by us and them, profit and purpose. Indeed, the urgent challenge for our times is to reimagine capitalism as a tool to enable our wholeness rather than to reinforce our separation. There could be no better blueprint for those of us who believe in the need for a moral revolution, and only those who are able to sidestep conformity traps can meet this challenge.

Chapter 9

USE THE POWER OF
MARKETS, DON'T
BE SEDUCED BY THEM

When I started Acumen in 2001, many prospective donors insisted we should be a for-profit fund. We were investing patient capital in mostly for-profit companies, they reasoned. If we used philanthropy to support for-profit investments, we would muddy the waters. At the same time, some nonprofit leaders flatly rejected out of hand the idea that we would use business as a tool for change. After a talk I gave in Bangladesh during Acumen's early days, an earnest young person accused me of being a "rapacious venture capitalist, earning money off the backs of the poor." That hurt. But, as I have learned, making all sides uncomfortable can be a signal that you are on to something.

I hear echoes of a similar conversation between generations. The older generation, especially those who lived in state-dominated economies like those in Eastern Europe, China, Russia, India, and large parts of Africa, remember lives of limited choices and opportunities and tend to favor free markets. The younger generation, who experienced the financial crisis of 2008, a calamity fueled by unbridled greed, convincingly points to the ravages of capitalism: inequality, divisiveness, climate change. Each group clings to its own version of reality.

Let me make a plea for nuance.

On the one hand, markets, the part of the economy that fulfills the needs of customers with products and services provided by businesses, have a fundamental role to play in healthy societies. At their best, markets efficiently allocate resources to meet the greatest demand. As long as individuals have access to them, markets give people control over their own lives rather than leaving them to the whims of government or charitable benefactors. Think of the massive emergence from poverty over the past thirty years, a billion people around the world supported by the opening of markets (along with interventions such as better health care and education).

On the other hand, if markets enable individual freedom, they also create inequality. Unchecked, capitalism overlooks or exploits those who cannot afford to pay; insufficiently considers the well-being of employees; and does not integrate onto balance sheets the cost of poorly utilizing earth's precious resources. The result is a profoundly unequal society in which the wealthiest feel above the system and the poorest feel left out altogether. In other words, capitalism without restraint is not good for any of us.

Moreover, when certain groups are barred from markets because of politics or prejudice, they can't participate fully in society. Remember Vimal, whose community was denied the opportunity to purchase a satellite dish for their televisions until he and his friends fought to be served? They weren't asking for favors, only access to markets as a form of freedom.*

---

* The economist and Nobel laureate Amartya Sen powerfully articulates the idea of access to markets as a form of freedom in his book *Development as Freedom*.

Knowing how to use and build markets is one of the most powerful tools we have for solving our problems. If you want to change even a small part of the world, learn to use the best of what markets can do while keeping them in their place. Resist the allure of short-term profit making, but don't reject the market entirely. Hold the tension. Use the market as a listening device (I explain this in chapter 4) and let it teach you what people value alongside what they can afford.

Indeed, the notion of the market as a listening device can be a powerful starting point for understanding both private and public problems. When Acumen first explored the issue of safe drinking water, a basic human need, we saw countless water filters designed to change the lives of the poor. But the inventors of those technologies often failed to let prospective clients' needs and tastes inform their designs.

Consequently, they learned far too late that people care a lot about their water's clarity, taste, and convenience, not to mention its price—in many urban and, increasingly, rural areas, the poor pay much more for water than their wealthy counterparts. Even if water is provided by the government, listening to poor "customers" is critical to any program's success. By failing to listen to the market, hundreds of billions of well-intentioned funding has gone down the drain.

In sectors such as energy, people with low incomes will pay for products and services when they see tangible gains on their investment. If I sell you an affordable solar light and, over time, save the money you would normally have doled out for kerosene, you are likely to tell your neighbors about it. That the solar light is cleaner, healthier, and significantly improves your lifestyle doesn't hurt, either.

But in other sectors, such as education, lower-income earners may not be able to afford what they need. If I offer early-childhood education facilities but charge enough tuition that the school at least breaks even, that leaves out the poor. I believe that every child in the world deserves an education that will allow them to contribute to the best of their abilities. So, does that mean public education is government's responsibility alone?

I used to confidently assert that the *only* way to enable fair opportunity to all children was to insist on public education for all—until I visited scores of schools in India and Pakistan. There, government-financed public schools are riddled with bureaucracy and corruption. Classrooms tend to be run-down and equipped with broken furniture or no furniture at all; and for the most part, neither teachers nor students show up for class. As a result, in Pakistan, 40 percent of low-income parents send their children to private schools. Low-income parents hungering to educate their children are willing to struggle and pay mightily for a better chance.

While we might demand that governments improve the quality of education for all children, how do we again hold the tension and use markets to build alternative models that serve the poor a high-quality product? By listening to the market, social entrepreneurs can identity what parents can afford to pay and then define the gap between that amount and the actual cost of delivering quality services. In the short term, philanthropy might fill that gap. But in the longer term, the only way to rectify the situation will be for government to step in.

Let's stand back from economic ideologies and start with the human problem we want to solve. We need a full understanding of the problem from the perspective of all stakeholders; only then can we determine the right kinds of capital (as well as the partnerships) needed to make the solution work. If you believe, as I do, that all human beings deserve access to affordable, quality education, to electricity, to primary health care, to a minimum level of clean drinking water and the like, then we need financial models that ensure universal access.

As I discussed earlier, Acumen has always seen its patient capital investments as a means to solving problems, not an end. In other words, the end or *purpose* of money is not simply to make more money, but to create something of value.

To place that in a moral framework: the more value our investments create, especially for the poor and vulnerable, the more we value our investments. Philanthropy enables us to take outsized risk—and time—investing in companies disrupting systems to serve the poor. Profits are a means to the sustainability of the innovations we support and, eventually, to ensuring that we also can cover our costs in the long term. Acumen's success hangs in the balance of two points on our moral compass, impact on one side and financial sustainability on the other.

Consider a complex issue like sanitation. People in the developed world take for granted having toilets that flush waste into enormous sewage treatment networks. In the developing world, however, 2.3 billion people rely on an outhouse or latrine, or else they defecate in the open air, which can lead to disease and often a loss of dignity.*

Indirectly, poor sanitation imposes a higher cost on women than on men. Schools that lack safe toilets typically see significant drop-out rates for girls once they begin menstruating, as they have no place to tend to their personal hygiene needs. And

---

* According to the WHO/UNICEF Joint Monitoring Programme for Water Supply, Sanitation and Hygeine's 2019 update report, *Progress on Household Drinking Water, Sanitation and Hygiene 2000–2017: Special Focus on Inequalities*, more than 4 billion people live without safely managed sanitation, even if some of them have access to a toilet.

rural areas lacking any toilets whatsoever force women to relieve themselves in fields, where they are vulnerable to violence from passersby.

Local governments, international aid agencies, and charities have all attempted unsuccessfully for decades to build latrines in slum areas. But without a plan to remove the waste and sustain the management of those toilets, the latrines quickly overflowed, creating stench and toxicity. No wonder traditional investors have stayed away from the business of providing toilets for the poor.

Solving such a complicated problem for one-third of the world's population could seem overwhelming—but not to David Auerbach, Lindsay Stradley, and Ani Vallabhaneni, who met at MIT's Sloan School of Management as graduate students and went on to found Sanergy. The three had each lived and worked in low-income communities, and they understood the connections between poor sanitation and diarrhea, cholera, and other water-borne diseases in slum areas especially.

The Sanergy founders were agnostic as to whether to take a for-profit or nonprofit approach to the problem; what mattered was solving it. In 2010, they traveled to Nairobi, Kenya, and found a smallish slum community of about forty thousand people where they could immerse themselves in learning and experimentation until they found a solution that worked. They used the market as a listening device, and considered every stakeholder group.

Mukuru, like the rest of Nairobi's slums, was known for "flying toilets," the practice of defecating on paper inside one's home and then tossing the bundle onto rooftops outside. The Sanergy founders met with many residents there who were willing to pay for a better, cleaner solution, especially as they were already in the habit of paying to use filthy toilets as a last resort. Individual entrepreneurs saw business opportunities in the owning and operating of toilets, and Mukuru, like all of Kenya, needed good jobs to employ its youth. Building a network of clean and sustainable toilets there made sense.

But before Sanergy could begin operating, the team needed to find local entrepreneurs willing to extend trust to three foreigners who had not yet proven their business model. "We just kept showing up," cofounder Lindsay Stradley explained. "For weeks, we would go into the slums and talk to people, until we made it clear we weren't going anywhere. The problem of waste had gotten out of control in Mukuru, so people were desperate to try a new solution. Plus, the entrepreneurs we connected with saw a business opportunity for themselves that also would do good for the community."

Sanergy's business model seeks to create value out of waste. The company manufactures toilets and sells them to the entrepreneurs, or "franchisees," for about five hundred dollars per toilet (a cost financed mostly via microloans). Sanergy employees then collect the waste from the entrepreneurs on a daily basis and compost it. In the early years, the founders lacked an answer to one of their biggest questions: what to do with the waste once it was collected. Might the government and others eventually come to see it as a resource rather than simply a cost? That would depend on whether the company was able to turn the waste into fertilizer that met health standards and that local farmers would purchase. The team would gain insights only by starting.

The founders correctly assumed the franchisees would repay their loans on the toilets with proceeds from their customers. Still, as it turned out, Sanergy needed both grants and loans before they could build a whole system to move waste effectively. They used grants to advertise their new service to local residents and for research into how best to compost and convert the waste into useful, salable products.

I visited Sanergy's office in Mukuru on a Sunday afternoon in October 2015. The slum's narrow entry road was lined with tarpaulin-covered kiosks crammed willy-nilly. Alleyways snaked between ricky-ticky houses made of mud, with open sewers running alongside. Lines of colorful laundry hung among the houses like prayer flags, and children were dressed in their finest clothing from a morning spent at church. A little girl reminded me of a princess from a Velázquez painting, her delicate hand daintily holding up her long, silky, scalloped blue skirt to avoid its becoming soiled.

Lindsay Stradley met me at Sanergy's small but lively office, which was filled with young people from around the world. She had just had her first child, but still came daily to the office to meet with local toilet entrepreneurs, solve problems with them, and grow the business. To show me Sanergy's business in action, she led me out of the office, striding in front of me through the muddy streets wearing jeans and bright yellow rubber boots, a huge smile on her face, clearly in her element.

We stopped in front of one of the toilet kiosks to meet Leah Gachanga, a square-jawed businesswoman with soft brown eyes. A colorful scarf was wrapped around her head. Leah proudly told me that she'd already grown her enterprise from one to three toilets, netting about five dollars per day on top of what she and her husband earned running a clothing store. Lindsay and I stood outside the bright blue toilet units with "Fresh Life" (Sanergy's local brand) painted in yellow on the sides. Just outside the units, Leah had set up a vanity station, complete with a mirror and washing stand. Like all Fresh Life agents, she charged about five cents per use for adults, two cents for children. She took care to clean the toilet after each customer left, and each day, young men in Fresh Life uniforms arrived to collect the waste in sealed containers, leaving the toilets fresh and odorless.

Leah relayed how much she loved contributing to her community. "Before Sanergy," she told me, "there was so much human waste right outside our houses. We would walk home, especially in the rainy season, and mud would rise so high that your boots became covered in an awful mix. Now the pathways are clean. Disease has fallen. I'm helping to make my community cleaner, and that makes me proud." Moreover, her efforts have changed the prospects for her family. "My customers have provided me with enough income to buy a home and educate my children in good schools," she said. "Fresh Life is good for all of us."

Lindsay and I continued walking along alleyways to the composting unit. Though Sanergy had been operating for several years by then and had seen significant interest from local farmers in its fertilizer, the company still lacked the European equivalent of FDA approval verifying that the product met health standards. When approved, the fertilizer delivery service would create good jobs and play a vital role in the community's health, culture, and business environment.

Lindsay, David, and Ani had focused maniacally on building a sustainable company that could solve a critical problem and, over the long term, provide a positive return to shareholders. But what they needed at that moment were patient investors who shared their values and aspirations. Though many loved the vision, most investors still wanted proof of the company's profitability before they would consider making a bet on Sanergy. The proof would only come later, making it all the more critical for the Sanergy founders to find investors who understood markets, yet also were willing to experiment and learn what it would take to build a sustainable, impactful model for change.

For patient investors, Sanergy's impact is significant. By March 2019, Sanergy had sold more than 2,500 toilets to local entrepreneurs, created more than 2,750 jobs, and provided affordable, hygienic sanitation services to more than 100,000 people, removing in excess of 6,000 tons of waste each year. That's about 600 big dump trucks full of human waste, which is composted and converted into organic fertilizer before being sold to commercial and smallholder farms. Major corporations interested in selling organic food products recently expressed interest in the fertilizer, which would bring the company's supply chain full circle.

Mukuru has been the main beneficiary of Sanergy's work. Disease rates have fallen, and education rates for adolescent girls have risen, as young women now have safe, private toilets to use at school. Community members feel a deep sense of pride in their homes, a benefit that matters, even if it is not always easy to measure.

The Sanergy founders have built a model that works, and are now looking to partner and grow the business significantly. Thrillingly, the city of Nairobi is interested in joining with the company to bring sanitation to all people. And the company continues to raise both grant money for research and development *and* investor capital.

Within eight years, Sanergy has become an example for patient investors, smart philanthropists, and city governments that are serious about solving a significant public health issue. The company's founders dreamed of providing a blueprint that governments could use to deliver "off-grid waste management," enabling the world's urban poor to improve their health, comfort, and dignity. Using moral imagination, the right kind of capital, and a circular business model that seriously considered all stakeholders, Sanergy's intrepid founders have succeded in turning waste into gold.

The more you understand how markets work, the better you'll be able to put markets in their place. The more you gain the tools needed to build financial viability into any endeavor you pursue, the more effectively you can solve intractable problems. Understanding markets is also critical to seeing and correcting some of the intrinsic flaws in our global economic system, blind spots that rely disproportionately on the toil and sweat of the working poor, holding them in a perennial cycle of indebtedness and impoverishment.

For example, agricultural markets have flourished for hundreds of years at the expense of the poorest farmers, the people who actually grow the food and drinks that nourish us. In Colombia, more than a half million smallholder farming families grow, pick, and export some of the finest coffee on earth. Yet the vast majority of these farmers live in poverty, often unable to cover the costs of production.

In 2009, Tyler Youngblood, a freelance writer and coffee enthusiast, found his imagination ignited by the rich, wet, emerald hills of Colombia's coffee-growing region. His curiosity drove him to meet everyone he could in the coffee industry and learn as much as possible about Colombian coffee production and its markets. His empathy for the coffee farmers urged him to ask: why was it so hard for them to make a living?

Almost everyone Tyler met pointed to the complicated global supply chain for coffee, which has been in place for at least a century. Millions of farmers grow coffee beans of varying qualities, then handpick the coffee cherries and sell them to domestic buyers and exporters at prices determined by global coffee futures. The exporters sell the coffee to roasters abroad, who in turn sell bags of high-priced coffee beans and lattes to the end consumer.

Why, Tyler wondered, were farmers beholden to a daily global commodities price, which was known for wild swings (from under a dollar to three dollars per pound) and had little to do with the realities of their production costs, when consumers paid the same amount for lattes regardless of commodity prices? Why, in an age of transparency, given that 25 million of the world's poorest citizens grew 80 percent of coffee produced, wasn't there a more ethical way to organize the industry?

Imagine being a farmer who drudges for months each season, investing your savings and time and not knowing what you will be paid until the day you deliver your harvest. You want to be able to sell your produce at fair prices. Ideally, you'd like "fair" to be a price that not only covers your costs but rewards your hard work with a commensurate financial return or profit. This is not what most coffee farmers experience. The majority of Colombian coffee farmers operate at a net financial loss. No wonder the average smallholder farmer is fifty-seven years old—most farmers' children decidedly do not want to become farmers.

Tyler dreamed of designing a system that started from the farmers' perspective. He knew this would entail ensuring a supply chain that compensated farmers fairly while also delivering a premium product to consumers. Isn't that the real point of markets, anyway, to ensure a fair and reasonable exchange of goods in ways that create value for all parties involved?

The result of Tyler's inquiry is Azahar, a coffee company that makes the markets work for farmers as well as everyone else along the supply chain. The company buys coffee directly from smallholder farmers because single-origin beans yield higher prices from international buyers. To ensure just pricing, Azahar works to understand farmers' costs of production and negotiates a long-term, fixed-price contract with roasters. These contracts between farmers and Azahar can yield prices two times higher than the global commodities price.

In return for their partnership, Azahar insists on the highest level of integrity from the farmers—timely delivery and no mixing of different qualities of beans. The company is able to pay so much more for the beans because it has developed a network of sustainable coffee consumers who want to know who is growing their coffee and how those people are treated. When I was in Colombia in November 2018, the world price was just about one dollar per pound; Azahar was paying the farmers, on average, two dollars per pound. The well-paid farmers are loyal to the company and consistently deliver the highest-quality beans.

I witnessed this sense of shared prosperity in 2017, when Acumen's Latin America director, Virgilio Barco, and I traveled to Nariño, in the southwest part of Colombia, bordering Ecuador and the Pacific Ocean. The land around Nariño is rich, verdant, and productive, perfect for growing coffee. Yet, like the Arhuacos who cultivate cacao in the north, the farmers who grow coffee in the southern region suffered greatly during the fifty-year civil war. Azahar was changing not only daily realities but future possibilities.

In Nariño, we met with a group of men and women farmers who had participated in an early revenue-sharing experiment with Azahar. Long, lonely hours toiling in the sun had carved creases of austerity and weariness into their faces. Most of the farmers stood quietly in a circle wearing jeans and cowboy hats, their eyes cast downward. Tyler, dressed in a white button-down shirt and jeans, his longish brown hair behind his ears and scholarly glasses perched above a mischievous smile, broke their silence with a simple hello. Then all eyes turned to him as he explained that thanks to an American buyer, each farmer would receive a bonus for the harvest based on additional premiums to be paid by the company.

One by one, the farmers approached the group's accountant, who sat on a simple stool in front of a small wooden table, checking handwritten ledger paper for the amount of beans each farmer had delivered. The farmers accepted the bonus in cash, usually with a wide grin, as the group applauded proudly.

I asked one of the men what he would do with his new income. "I'm saving to buy more land," he said. Tyler explained that for the first time, Colombian smallholders see the potential to earn a good living in coffee, but only if they own more than two hectares—and most farmers in Colombia own less.

"You seem happy today," I said to a cluster of farmers. "But is this company really different from the other coffee buyers?"

"Azahar cares about us," one farmer responded. He had jet-black eyes and a thick fringe of hair to match. "They aren't here just to make money from us, but to help *us* earn money, too. We trust them."

"Our *job* is to build a community of trust," Tyler explained to Virgilio and me over dinner that evening. "Specialty coffee depends on a supply chain with trust at every link. Our buyers depend on us to sell them single-origin beans with no mistakes; they need to trust that we will deliver the highest-quality coffee. Our customers need to trust that our farmers are paid sustainably. And our farmers need to trust that we will adhere to our fixed agreement, paying the best prices in a timely manner. They need to know that we will show up. We have to do this outside a traditional commercial or legal framework. We have to do it because it is the right thing to do."

The phrase a "community of trust" resonates; it unites the many stakeholders of social enterprise, linking the hands and minds of those who produce and deliver our daily bread and everything else we use. The reality of creating such a community is another story. Many peers and investors think Tyler and others like him are insane to pay double the world coffee price.

Tyler took a conventional economic model and turned it upside down, understanding that farmers needed to be fully included in the supply chain, not as inputs but as dignified human beings whose long months of work produced daily cups of joy for the world. It took the courage and creativity of nonconformity to build a business based on the production costs of the farmers, not on maximizing sales to the buyers. It took persistence fueled by a belief that trust, empathy, and mutual accountability are the bedrock of healthy societies.

In November 2018 we met Tyler again, this time at a hip yet elegant retail Azahar store in a popular section of Bogotá. Every table was filled with residents talking, working, and drinking Azahar's fine coffee. "When I got here in 2010," Tyler said, "Colombians couldn't find much high-quality coffee from their own country to drink. All the good stuff was exported. It feels good to be part of changing that."

Market fundamentalists may ask how entrepreneurs such as the founders of Sanergy and Azahar make good decisions while balancing multiple bottom lines. With the single metric of profit, the results are binary: you are either profitable or not. But profit doesn't take into account the natural resources we consume, the pollution we create, and the employees we empower. Nor does it grapple with issues of fairness that operate in systems with wildly unbalanced power dynamics. The shareholder capitalist system also does not value the social and environmental capital some businesses are creating (which, in some cases, is enormous), focusing only on short-term profitability. But human beings created the current systems that govern our lives. It is up to human beings to change and evolve those systems.

The current economic system keeps the attention on what we can count (profits) rather than on what we most value (our children's health and education, the quality of the air we breathe, just compensation to the poorest, etc.). Companies and investors tend to allocate financial and human resources to achieve the highest possible financial returns, and even some impact investors count it as a bonus rather than a requirement when social impact is also achieved. The expense of corporate resources on fairly integrating smallholder farmers into the supply chain, training women and minorities, and protecting and strengthening the environment tends to be relegated to Corporate Social Responsibility or philanthropy. Yet, only when companies regularly quantify and *value* nonpecuniary but fundamental human and environmental benefits will we see a more inclusive, sustainable market system.

Like many of our peers, the team at Acumen and I have been working for many years to develop new approaches to measuring social impact as a complement to quantitative financial analysis. In Acumen's early years, like most socially oriented organizations, we counted "outputs" (the number of toilets produced, the number of people trained or jobs created). That approach gave us a sense of scale, but it fell short of showing whether our companies were effective at helping people lift themselves from poverty. And we wanted to hold ourselves, and our companies, accountable for doing just that.

The cell phone revolution led to the ability to communicate with thousands of low-income customers simultaneously. In 2015, building on the work of others, Acumen developed Lean

Data, an approach to measuring impact using cell phones. Using this approach, Acumen can simultaneously text thousands of customers of a given project or company, asking a series of questions from which we then deduce invaluable information such as income level and whether using a certain product has had a positive or negative impact on its user. We learn what people value, or don't, about a specific project. Low-income customers answer these questions very seriously, so that companies know how to serve them based on what they actually need, not what we *think* they need. Lean Data is a step forward in treating the poor as customers, not victims.

For example, remember the solar lighting company d.light from chapter 4? Acumen has invested more than thirty million dollars in companies like d.light that are bringing off-grid solar electricity to low-income people around the world. We hope to realize financial returns yet do not expect to compete with traditional venture capitalists on a returns basis alone. Instead, we are counting on our portfolio of companies to bring measurable change to the lives of many. Our energy companies, reaching well over 110 million and counting—does not disappoint.

Consider these results. Lean Data surveys have demonstrated that solar light results in low-income people staying active an extra hour each night. Children study about an hour more as well. Customers tend to place high value on the security and peace of mind that electricity brings—harder to quantify but important. Our investments also have kept more than seven million tons of carbon dioxide and black carbon from being released into the atmosphere. Over one hundred million lives are better. And most important, we *know* in what ways those lives have improved because the people living with the solar products have told us so.

Imagine if more of us allocated our resources, placing

social and environmental impact on an equal footing with (or higher than) financial returns. Everything would change.

Using markets without being seduced by them does not require a degree in rocket science, but it does require fortitude to move beyond a profit-alone mentality. The process starts with focusing first on purpose; considering all stakeholders; using the right kind of capital; hiring competent, values-aligned talent; and measuring what matters, not just what you can count. We are the ones who choose the kind of economy and society we inhabit. We can continue to play by tired rules that work only for the few, at the expense of the many, or we can imagine and build new rules that work for everyone. It is all within our individual and collective grasp.

Chapter 10

PARTNER WITH HUMILITY AND AUDACITY

If you want to create or renew systems, small is beautiful but scale is critical. Changing systems for the poor, not just the rich, requires understanding how to use markets and how to partner with government, which means moving from small-scale purity to the messy and complex thickness of scale. I'm not talking about growth for growth's sake though. Rather, I'm underscoring the need to recognize the problem you are solving and then executing a strategy to either replicate your business model or partner to expand your model's reach. Neither path is easy. But if you are up to the challenge, you could enable widespread transformation.

In the summer of 2007, I was speaking at the Aspen Ideas Festival to a crowd of a couple hundred wealthy people, mostly Americans, about Acumen's latest investment, an ambulance company in India. The Indian government was spending more than a billion dollars annually on emergency services, yet in Mumbai (the country's financial center and largest city), only a few emergency service units actually functioned. At that time, the emergency medical sector across India was notoriously bloated and corrupt; 90 percent of people traveling in ambulances were already dead and en route to the morgue. It was common knowledge that if you wanted to get to the hospital quickly, you were much better off calling a taxi.

Earlier that year, Acumen's India team had invested in Ziqitza, a social enterprise with the singular mission of disrupting the emergency services industry in India. The company had begun operating with nine ambulances as a purely private business: 80 percent of clients paid market prices to be transported to private hospitals. The company made a deliberate commitment to ensure that the other 20 percent of its clients were low-income people who paid only what they could afford.

We knew that the risks of disrupting such a massive industry were enormous, but the combination of the inclusive business model and the commitment of the founders reinforced our conviction in making the investment.

Under that white tent in Aspen, one of India's most eminent businessmen raised his hand to ask a question.

"I applaud your ambition," the great man said. "But did I hear you correctly? Nine ambulances? Mumbai is a city of seventeen million people [by 2019, more than twenty-two million]. Are you seriously backing a group with only nine ambulances?" The businessman continued, his doleful lament by then so familiar that I could have filled in the words myself. "This is the problem with social enterprises. They are mediocre businesses run by smart, idealistic people and have no hope of changing anything except at a small-scale level. This sideline approach distracts from the real issues and takes pressure off government from doing their job."

My face flushed. The businessman's statement felt like censure, a personal rebuke made public in front of my peers at an esteemed institution where I served as a trustee. I sensed a wave of doubt about our model sweeping the audience. Heads nodded in unison.

A snippet from a Mary Oliver poem arose inside me like a good friend: "Let me keep my distance, always, from those / who think they have the answers." Bring on the skeptics—we need them—but those of us who want a better world have little use for critics who armor themselves with rigid certainty, especially if they propose neither assistance nor solutions.

"At least we're trying," I said, "and nothing else seems to be working. Why would we *not* try?" I was a believer in social enterprise precisely because the big players who dominated systems rarely had the creativity, daring, or nimbleness needed to disrupt the status quo. Yet I wasn't certain that we would succeed. Indeed, the odds were against this company. But Ziqitza would learn only by trying. And so would we.

That day in Aspen, I wish I'd known then what I understand now: that visionary builders who reshape entire industries perceive the big picture while working to get their initial operating model right, even if that model starts out small. These audacious individuals must possess the character to withstand naysayers and bullies.

Of course the founders of Ziqitza started small. As with Jawad in his dream of affordable housing in Pakistan, they were out to build something that had not succeeded in India prior to their efforts. The group required time to experiment and fail until they discovered how to run a high-quality ambulance service with a decidedly social objective. Once the model was in place, the company could then more easily partner with government to reach a scale that served millions.

While I was less articulate in that Aspen tent than I would have liked, a number of factors persuaded me that my team at Acumen had made the right bet on Ziqitza.

First, the founders had started their business to solve a problem with which they had a deep sense of personal connection. Years earlier, in the southern Indian state of Kerala, Shaffi Mather, one of Ziqitza's five founders and its team leader, had nearly lost his mother when she woke up choking and couldn't find anything but a taxi to take her to the hospital. Around that same time, the mother of Shaffi's cofounder Ravi Krishna was traveling in New York City when she collapsed on the sidewalk. Ravi's mother's companion called 911, and within minutes they were met by trained medical personnel who provided effective assistance on the spot, saving Ravi's mother's life. Why, the founders reasoned, shouldn't India's people expect a similar response?

Second, when the time came to scale up the business, the Ziqitza cofounders would be ready. Like Shaffi and Ravi, the other cofounders, Sweta Mangal, Naresh Jain, and Manish Sacheti, had experience working in different divisions of large corporations, learning to manage talent, build effective supply chains, and grow technology businesses. They knew how to lay the groundwork for scale.

And, last, we at Acumen believed in the character of the founders. Shaffi Mather reminded me of a bull in a china shop, filled with the right kind of ambition, enthusiasm, and energy, if not always with grace and mindfulness.

If anyone could pull off a major disruption in a broken industry, this guy and his partners could, even if they did not yet fully understand their project's exact path to growth.

When I told Shaffi about the Indian businessman's disparaging remarks, he simply shrugged. "You know what Gandhi said about society-changing innovations?" he asked. "First, they ignore you. Then they laugh at you. Then they fight you. Then you win."

But if vision, the right skills, *and* character got Ziqitza to the starting block, the Indian businessman's question nonetheless dogged me. I wondered how the company would raise additional investment capital, given its commitment to providing 20 percent of its customers with a significant subsidy. We had invested because Ziqitza was dedicated to an inclusive business model. Yet how, I wondered, could we protect our investment to serve the poor while supporting the company's clear need to grow financially?

In the early years, the company grew organically, serving thousands of low-income people who'd never before had access to ambulance services. That was a good start, but given our focus on the poor, the company wasn't reaching enough low-income people to justify our large stake. A few well-intentioned potential investors suggested that it would do better financially and reach more people overall if it targeted a higher income bracket and removed the requirement to serve low-income people.

"You can always go down-market once you've built a viable model," one American investor told me.

True, I thought, but how many years would that take? The idea sounded too much like business as usual: serve the wealthy and give back through the side door only once you're flush with profits. Ziqitza had at the core of its business a vision to serve all people, and we needed to do what we could do to protect that vision while also helping the company expand.

In 2008, a year after I spoke at Aspen, an established U.S.-based emergency services company explored purchasing a significant share of Ziqitza, sensing its long-term financial potential. Though thrilled to see such interest, I worried about whether this more profit-oriented entity would agree to devoting 20 percent of its services to the poor. The next morning, I called Shaffi, and he agreed that Ziqitza would change its bylaws to make explicit the company's commitment to serving the poor before any shares were sold. That bylaw change strengthened trust between Acumen and Ziqitza. We were both learning to build for purpose *and* profitability.

Then, tragedy. On November 26, 2008, I was celebrating Thanksgiving, my favorite holiday, with my family in New York when a teammate called and told me to turn on CNN: Mumbai was under siege from terrorists. The Taj and Oberoi hotels, two of the city's finest, were burning; people were trapped inside and many were believed dead (in total, 174 were killed and more than 300 wounded). I couldn't believe this was happening in my beloved Mumbai. Tears streamed as I watched footage of desperate, terrified people running through smoky streets.

Next, to my amazement, there appeared in front of every burning building, bright yellow ambulances—*our* ambulances—each equipped with capable medical personnel and all the up-to-date technology required to respond to the acute needs of disaster victims.

The ambulance drivers, I later learned, ran headlong into the burning buildings, despite the presence of terrorists killing anyone in their path. Somehow, every driver survived while rescuing more than a hundred of the terrorists' intended victims. Lives were saved because of this little company—and everyone in our global community felt part of it. For all of this, thanksgiving.

A few months after the tragedy, I shared a simple lunch with the ambulance drivers on the rooftop of the company's office at the edge of Mumbai. I asked a driver who was relatively short in stature but of sturdy build what had made him act so courageously on the day of the attacks.

"There was too much need," he said. "When the commandos came, I followed them into the hotel. We saw the attackers with their guns firing. A commando pushed me to a corner where I would not be seen by the terrorists. We waited for the terrorists to move to another room and then we pulled wounded people out of the hotel. There were so many people in pain. So, we went back in. We came back the next day and the next day, too."

I praised the driver's humility, and asked again how he had stared down the threat of death and acted anyway.

He answered, "I'm a driver who can help save lives. It is my duty to do so, madam."

Here was a man who earned just a few dollars a day. His character was a reflection of the company that valued and nurtured character in every employee. To me, his courage made him a giant.

I wasn't alone in being moved by the effectiveness of the company. Though still relatively small, it managed a swift, competent response, earning the respect of Indian bureaucrats charged with bringing public emergency health services to their states. Soon, Ziqitza was invited to compete for state government contracts to provide free ambulance services. In pursuing these tenders, it could now point to its track record as well as its ethics.

Thus began the company's transformation into a private-public partnership, and to a level of growth that would eventually make it one of the largest emergency service companies in the world. As of 2019, Ziqitza operates more than 3,600 ambulances, employs 12,000 people, and has delivered more than 4 million patients to hospitals. Moreover, by moving from a private-sector company to partnering with the government, it was able to extend its services to those who previously were excluded from the emergency health care system altogether. In 2014, Acumen did a Lean Data study of two of the states where Ziqitza was operating and found that more than 75 percent of those served were poor, an almost complete flip of the client ratio when the company was private.

But that impressive scale and the company's increasing inclusiveness came neither easily nor without a cost. To make such growth possible, Ziqitza's leaders needed the humility to stare down the realities of their business. That may seem oxymoronic, but the opposite approach would be to assume that you can simply build a better service or product and watch the world beat a path to your door. Humility is needed to recognize the barriers in your way. Audacity is key to imagining a different future regardless, firing up the resolve to overcome impediments to your goal.

For Ziqitza, those realities included the complacency and bureaucracy that often go hand in hand with doing business with governments. In March 2019 in Acumen's Mumbai office, Shaffi and I had a long talk about government. He said there are "good officials, bad officials, and indifferent ones."

Ziqitza cofounder Sweta Mangal tells the story of dealing with one particularly vexing official who demanded a 5 percent "fee" each month before he would process the government payment, which the company needed to pay its employees. The company refused.

"Each month, he would delay," Sweta said. "That delay would result in us being slower to pay our drivers and other workers, who lacked any financial cushion to absorb even minor shocks. We would explain to our team that the late payments were due not to a lack of competence on our part, but because we stood by our values. The employees were proud to work for us, but some also reminded us that you can't eat values." Sweta added that those conversations humbled and hurt; and reinforced the founders' resolution to stay the course.

As the company continued to refuse to pay the bribes, the government official grew more aggressive, at one point calling Sweta to demand payment. He had apparently forgotten that ambulance companies record all phone calls.

You might think the shame of being recorded in the act of extortion would be enough to quell someone's appetite for corruption, and for a few months, demands for bribes ceased, at least from that one official. Then, at one point, the local government represented by that official accused *Ziqitza* of corruption, which we took very seriously at Acumen. There were times, in truth, when it would have been easier for Acumen to walk away, but we had signed up to be patient investors, partners in disruption. Moreover, we believed in government and the potential of the right private service providers such as Ziqitza to partner and make good on government's obligations to its citizens.

Some might ask, why even bother partnering with government when there are so many challenges and seductions?

First, government itself is not corrupt. Individuals may take advantage of systems that need improvement, but that doesn't mean that all people working in government are corrupt. As

Shaffi would say, you have to find "the good ones." And there are plenty of thoughtful, principled, courageous individuals in government doing what they can to change broken, corroded systems. They can be powerful change-makers and allies, so keep an eye out for them. You might also consider working in the public sector yourself.

Second, partnering with government is essential for getting quality health care to the rural poor. Markets alone will never succeed in protecting our most vulnerable from disease or misfortune, but companies such as Ziqitza can help government achieve its goals of serving its citizens and protecting its most vulnerable.

Eventually, Ziqitza came to know which government officials shared their values and which did not. The best local government agencies discussed their own challenges and problem-solved directly with the company. Over time, these various "good" partners and Ziqitza wove a web of trust that only intensified.

Our most disadvantaged communities could avoid many every day tragedies if our public systems were built on twin pillars of character and competence. I saw this in 2014, when visiting Ziqitza's branch office in Bhubaneswar, the capital of Odisha, one of India's three poorest states. Before Ziqitza's partnership with the local government, an older fisherman said to me as tears ran down his face, "I saw too many family members die when we had to use a bullock cart to get them from my village to the hospital. Now, the gods have come, madam. We can save ourselves."

I got the sense of a "before Ziqitza" and an "after Ziqitza" way of thinking and behaving.

Sumit Basu, the thirtysomething regional manager of

Ziqitza Odisha, recounted stories of a terrible cyclone that ripped through the state a year prior. "We had every ambulance at the ready," Sumit said. "Over two nights with the cyclone, the company's vehicles drove thirty-seven pregnant women to safety and delivered at least one healthy baby inside an ambulance. Not a single life was lost. Our region has seen great tragedies, and lost thousands due to cyclones in the past. But Ziqitza and the government were fully prepared this time. We worked together."

Solving humanity's toughest problems requires no single hero, but a *system* of people, companies, organizations, and government that rally around a common enterprise. Ziqitza could offer operational efficiencies and nimble decision making, but the company had to partner with government to reach millions of low-income people in need of their services. Government required the high standards, quality of service, and efficiencies delivered by the private company. Workers, whether manning call centers, driving ambulances, or serving as medical technicians, had to look beyond their own needs and operate from a sense of duty and service to the greater good. Ziqitza's rules and practices have now become the standard benchmarks for ambulance services across India.

The road to trust and effectiveness for Ziqitza was long and, at times, arduous. The company's story of creating and maintaining reliable, productive partnerships carries important lessons for every organization that wants to extend beyond what it does well on its own.

First and foremost, be clear about your purpose and honest about what you bring to the table, as well as what you hope to take away. Are you and your partner values-aligned and committed to learning together? Are you willing to compromise and be clear on those compromises, not in an easy "the ends justify the means" way, but in that gray area that recognizes the imperfection of the world—and of every human being? To create change, we have to be willing to be uncomfortable without losing sight of what is most important.

Partnering effectively takes time and commitment. If we believe that a moral revolution requires everyone, we must become skilled at building trusting partnerships across sectors. Honing this skill almost always requires a shift in both assumptions and behaviors. Nonprofits need to let go of suspicions that all corporations are greedy, exploitative, and unconcerned with the earth, while still holding to account those who are greedy and exploitative. For-profit companies must drop the assumption that all nonprofits are full of woolly headed, morally righteous do-gooders who get nothing done, while still calling on the carpet those who are ineffectual. And many of us must shift our lazy assumptions about other sectors, giving up presumptions about government ("corrupt and ineffective"), media ("liars"), philanthropy ("entitled and disconnected"), and technology ("monstrous and self-serving"). Of course, some people and organizations fit these assumptions, but when we refuse to see the humanity in those who share a desire to create change, we miss the chance to amplify our work and realize our mission. And we are all needed to build more just and inclusive societies in which each individual counts.

Yasmina Zaidman, Acumen's chief of strategic partnerships, wisely counsels, "If I could have one wish—and this is something I try to practice myself—it would be to enter a new partnership with greater openness to what the other side can offer and a courageous vulnerability to sharing fears—and with the patience to take the time it needs to build trust."

In other words, commit to the commitment itself.

Sometimes, what looks like a great partnership at first might ultimately let you down. My heart has been broken by corporations that told a good story of purpose, but in the end were focused on business as usual. One phrase I dread is "We want to be part of radical change as long as it doesn't impact shareholder value." That is a clear moment for pushback, or for a difficult conversation, at the very least. It is a chance to try to bring your would-be partner's focus back to the problem you're trying to solve together. If you cannot do that, you may need another partner.

If, however, you find a corporate partner that recognizes that its global supply chain is broken and wants to explore models to make it more inclusive and sustainable, try to support that partner as it fights its internal battles. As with government, some of the most courageous change agents I have met work in large corporations. They are aware of the risks involved in rejecting the status quo, but they do so anyway. For them, partnering with external allies staves off the solitude that comes from being a lone questioning voice and also helps them bolster the firm's legitimacy in delivering on its promises to stakeholders.

Some partnerships fail; it's part of life. If a partnership sounds too good to be true, it usually is. If donors insist that you "collaborate" with another organization whose mission or values do not seem aligned, spend time making sure that the misalignment truly exists, and then say no gracefully.

Be wildly cautious when an organization calls and says, "We love what you do. We should find ways to partner." If they cannot articulate why to partner, how to partner, or, most important, to what end, you won't have a partnership; you'll have a mess. Ironically, sometimes those you see as *least* like you may be exactly who you need for what you want to accomplish. So, start again with your mission and an understanding of which skills, markets, and communication outlets enable you to realize the good you are creating for those in need.

* * *

What if you are starting out with just a giant, uplifting and daring idea and no resources, networks, or money? How do you even begin to find the partners who can help you realize your goal? There are few better stories in my experience of impact investing than the one about a chicken company in Ethiopia that started out as a ragtag operation with founders who'd never before seen live chickens yet went on to change the fortunes of millions of poor farmers. Today, they are providing financial opportunities, improving health outcomes, transforming an industry, and in so doing, helping to strengthen a nation.

That story begins in 2009, when an American named Dave Ellis spent a year in Uganda working for a well-intentioned start-up NGO that never got off the ground. Most of the Ugandans he met wanted jobs, which convinced him that poverty would not be solved by an act of charity. The next year, encouraged to try something different, Dave and his partner, Joe Shields, traveled to Ethiopia, a country of one hundred million people, with a small amount of investment capital in search of a business that would enable them to make a greater difference.

Soon after arriving in Tigray, a region in northern Ethiopia near the border of Eritrea, Dave chanced upon the right opportunity: The government owned a six-hundred-thousand-square-foot defunct chicken operation and was looking for a partner to make it productive. The only problem was that it contained not a single healthy flock of chickens. Under past management, most of the chickens had died.

Though Dave had grown up in Chicago and had never encountered a live chicken, he was undaunted. The lease for the factory was within his financial reach, and the opportunity he saw was enormous. In the region of Tigray, an estimated 58 percent of children were malnourished. Eggs are an inexpensive form of protein, and chickens generate income. Moreover, a new generation of Ethiopian leaders was looking to partner with private-sector players to jump-start a flagging economy.

Unlike the cofounders of Ziqitza, the ambulance company that initially was private, Dave, Joe, and a third cofounder, Trent Koutsoubos, put their company into partnership with government from the start; they assumed that "all they had to do" was raise baby chicks to egg-laying age (forty-five to sixty days) and then sell them to government extension agents, who would be responsible for selling the chicks to smallholder farmers across the country. To fledgling entrepreneurs Dave and Joe, this plan sounded straightforward and easy.

The first night the entrepreneurs were on the farm with newly purchased chickens, two of the chicken houses caught on fire from an electrical malfunction, and the founders had to carry the frightened birds outside in their arms. Once things settled down, the company restarted operations and set a date with government extension workers to pick up a major order of baby chicks exactly thirty-five days after they were born.

The workers showed up with fifteen trucks—a month late. By then, the company founders had already scrabbled to sell the baby chicks to whomever they could find; this was another setback to operations, resulting in more lost money that the founders didn't have. As for the extension workers, they had no choice but to return to their posts with empty trucks. Trust on both sides plummeted.

Dented but undaunted, Dave and Joe went back to the

drawing board. The cofounders reviewed what had happened and reminded themselves of their purpose. They were in Ethiopia to build a successful chicken operation that would feed the poor and change the lives of farmers. They reconsidered their own strengths and weaknesses as well as those of their various partners.

Try. Fail. Learn. Start again.

This time, Dave and Joe tried selling one-day-old chicks directly to the farmers, but the farmers were both poor and overworked, earning on average $350 a year. Smallholders can afford to buy just a few chickens at a time, and they have multiple constraints that prevent them from finding the right vaccines, the most effective feed, and the means to keep the chickens safe at night, when predators such as foxes and dogs roam about looking for vulnerable, fluffy, chirping yellow snacks. In short, raising baby chicks from birth to forty-five days (after which they could thrive in a village environment) took time, money, and expertise, none of which the smallholders had.

Though operations faltered again, Dave and Joe were gaining a better sense of the farmers' and the government's potential as partners. While Ethiopia's state-run enterprises may have lacked some efficiencies, the government's agricultural extension workers, who knew and lived among smallholder farmers, were highly trusted. The government workers thus represented an enormous asset to the company—if Dave and Joe were willing to discern those functions where government workers were most capable of delivering. Dave explained: "We saw that we could work with local government offices to mobilize demand for the chickens and educate the farmers. The government also helped us reach last-mile areas we could never reach ourselves."

So, the cofounders changed the model again. The company, which Dave and Joe named EthioChicken, now breeds chickens and incubates eggs, selling them a day after they're born in batches of one thousand to "agents," individual entrepreneurs who raise the chicks for the next forty-five to sixty days. EthioChicken provides the agents with the vaccines, feed, and other supplies along with the inputs and advice they require to succeed. Then the agents help the farmers by selling three to four chickens at a time in collaboration with government extension workers. Once the chickens are at egg-laying age, they stay close to home and eat most anything, making them the perfect investment for a poor farmer.

In August 2017, Dave and I met Yohannes, a nineteen-year-old who had signed up to serve as an agent, raising the tiny chicks until they'd grown old enough to sell to individual farmers. We stood together in the corrugated tin shed Johannes had constructed to house two thousand chicks. Wearing wraparound sunglasses, a black watch, a white lab coat, and an amulet around his neck, Yohannes waved his delicate, long-fingered hands enthusiastically as he shared with me his success. A couple of years prior, he'd taken a loan from a local microfinance organization to purchase his first batch of a thousand chicks. "I knew that I had to keep those chicks healthy and alive," he told us. "I slept in the room with them every night. EthioChicken gave me advice, and the government helped me until I could sell all the chickens. Now I am a happy man. All my brothers and sisters go to school and are happy, too."

We'd been speaking for a good half hour before Yohannes shared that he'd taken a risk with the company because his life depended on it. He and his five younger siblings had been orphaned, and the teenage Yohannes was responsible for their collective welfare. His risk and diligence paid off: by the end of 2017, he had sold fifteen thousand chickens, all to small-holder farmers. That year, his earnings exceeded ten thousand dollars, an astronomical sum in a country where most people earn a dollar a day.

In 2019, EthioChicken sold over 1.5 million one-day-old chicks every month to 5,500 agents who earned anywhere from $1,000 to $10,000 a year. The agents sell to about 4 million farmers, who represent nearly 25 million family members. By our estimates, EthioChicken is annually injecting more than $200 million into Ethiopia's economy. The company has grown to 1,200 employees, all but 4 of them Ethiopian. In the five-million-person region of Tigray, where EthioChicken started, malnutrition rates have fallen more than 11 percent. The government credits EthioChicken with much of that gain in nutrition, and it has integrated chicken rearing into its overall agricultural strategy.

EthioChicken learned to partner—with the government, with agents, with Acumen as an investor, and with charities such as the Gates Foundation. Each of these partners brought something different to this enterprise, while remaining committed to the same goal. Getting EthioChicken on its feet may have taken longer than either Dave or Joe thought it would when they started, but by partnering with government, the company helped make Ethiopia a model for empowering smallholder farmers with chickens and their eggs as a source of both income and protein.

What struck me most about Dave's and EthioChicken's approach to partnering was, again, not only the audacity of their vision, but the quality of their humility and, therefore, their ability to build trust. Dave speaks openly about the mistakes the company made when he and Joe first arrived in Ethiopia.

He recognizes that they initially assumed they had the answers, rushing to share what they themselves were bringing to the table. They first had to listen more closely to what the government needed in order to help its people—and only then act.

Dave and Joe also realized that they could not partner alone effectively. They needed the assistance of people such as Dr. Fseha Tesfu, their soft-spoken but resilient Ethiopian national sales manager, who manages EthioChicken's relationship with government. On the government side, the state minister for livestock, Dr. Gebregziabher Gebreyohannes, was a believer in the company's potential from its early days, backing them up as they hit inevitable speed bumps along the path to success. After all, *individuals*, not institutions, create the relationships that lead to change.

Dave models building trust with those at all levels of an institution, and all kinds of stakeholders. I have watched him interact with agents, farmers, and extension workers with enormous humility, shaking everyone's hand; speaking in Ethiopia's official tongue, Amharic; eating the local food with the exuberance he brings to everything; and praising the goodness he has discovered in his adopted country. In never forgetting that you are a guest, you are more likely to be accepted as a local.

In 2014, recognizing the company's ability to deliver, Ethiopia's Southern Nations, Nationalities, and Peoples' Region offered EthioChicken a contract to take over two more failing farms, this time on a fixed-payment arrangement. "I don't think we would have been as successful without working with the Ethiopian government," Dave told me. "The government allowed us to build trust very quickly with smallholder farmers. And to build a market that has changed the game."

I was recently asked if it was possible to teach people to

build trust. Yes, I believe so. Given that trust is our rarest currency, we have no choice but to teach our children, and one another, to be trusting and worthy of trust. You build trust by showing up, by listening to what someone else has to say, by keeping promises. You build trust through shared endeavor and by the consistency of your words and actions. You build it by admitting mistakes and by communicating both when things go well and when they fail. You build trust by knowing your values, living them, and being clear with others that you will not violate those values.

Most of our grandmothers could have given us this same advice.

Chapter 11

ACCOMPANY EACH OTHER

In 1987, while I was building Duterimbere, I also helped a group of unwed mothers transform a charity project into a bakery business. I'd recognized that too few microentrepreneurs in Rwanda employed people beyond a couple of family members, so I decided to try my hand at building a business, foolishly assuming the endeavor would be easy. The women already knew how to bake, and there was a ready market in the fancier offices in town. Moreover, there was no real competition at the time.

But in the beginning, no matter how hard I tried to make things work, we failed. The women didn't show up on time. They stole from the bakery. They were too fearful to knock on office doors and introduce themselves, looking at the floor when anyone spoke to them. The women had few marketable skills, no trust, and little entrepreneurial drive. It took me a while to identify the entanglement of forces that kept these women from taking advantage of this "market opportunity." They were from poor families, and most were illiterate and unskilled, divided from mainstream society and divorced from their own sense of worth.

So-called "respectable people" kept their distance from such poverty, referring to the poor women as "prostitutes" and seeing them as second-class citizens, at best. The poor and vulnerable continually suffer from poverty's many forms of violence: dangerous physical environments, miserable schools, inadequate health care, and untrustworthy courts. In turn, many poor and vulnerable people inflict a further sense of unworthiness on themselves. I began to understand what Rousseau meant when he wrote in *The Social Contract* that "man is born free, yet everywhere he is in chains."

Intuitively, I adjusted the role I played, no longer simply a manager, but a coach, a cheerleader, a friend. Each Friday, I'd hold sessions to teach the women how business worked in ways that connected to *their* realities, not mine. We practiced saying hello to strangers. I joined them to try to convince shopkeepers to stock our baked goods. I was at the bakery most mornings when they arrived, and we celebrated small victories together. And sometimes we laughed, joyfully and boisterously. Their challenges in the bakery became mine to solve not *for* them but *with* them.

Though frustrated daily, I found that I liked the person I was when I was around these women. I discovered ways to hold a mirror to their inner beauty and potential, and they reflected back to me the best parts of myself. Appreciation revealed itself in an unexpected smile, a hug, or a collective cheer when our sales finally began to creep upward and the number of stolen goods declined to zero. Yet our shared journey was more than one of mutual gratitude. In time, the women began to earn more than most of their peers while building a business, seeing a steady income, and establishing self-esteem. Finally, they had unearthed a sense of dignity inside themselves that no one could take away from them.

Without knowing it, I was learning to practice the principle of accompaniment.

Accompaniment is a Jesuit idea, meaning to "live and walk" alongside those you serve. It is the willingness to encounter another, to make someone feel valued and seen, bettered for knowing you, never belittled. Guiding another person, organization, or community to build confidence and capabilities requires tenacity, a disciplined resolve to show up repeatedly with no expectation of thanks in return. This kind of accompaniment requires the patience to listen to others' stories without judgment, to offer skills and solutions without imposition. It is to be a follower as well as a guide, a humble yet aspirational teacher-student focused on coaching another with firm kindness and a steady presence. With those you aim to serve or lead, your job is to be *interested*, to help make another person shine, not demonstrate how smart or good or capable you yourself are.

Accompaniment is especially important when partnering with those who are from places or families that have been traumatized or marginalized by war, violence, isolation, aggression, or by drugs or generational poverty. Accompaniment recognizes that for many individuals and communities, spiritual poverty is as devastating as material poverty. The simple act of showing up and connecting with another's humanity can help a person rekindle hope in ways they might not otherwise have dreamed of doing.

Think of someone in your own life who saw the best version of who *you* could be, even when you couldn't see that version yourself. That person could be a parent, sibling, mentor, teacher, coach, or boss who dared you, pushed you, equipped you with the skills to succeed; a friend who told you hard truths constructively, perhaps with toughness but bolstered by determined love, all with the end result of making you feel bigger, more awake, more *here*. If you can think of just one person who accompanied you like that, you should count yourself lucky.

Now think of the people who feel left out—those living in poverty, in conflict areas, sitting in prison, or struggling in refugee camps. Many in those communities are exposed to endless callousness and constant criticism. Often, they internalize the perceptions that others impose on them—that they are predatory, parasitic, unfit, unworthy, or invisible.

Despair is not the singular domain of the poor. For all of us who have suffered unimaginable loss or who are in crisis or physical pain, just getting out of bed can sometimes be an act of courage. For anyone experiencing loneliness or despondency, there is great power in knowing that while you have to do the hard work of change on your own, someone out there has your back.

I've always been drawn to businesses that integrate the spirit of accompaniment into their operations. I moved to Africa in 1986 because I'd seen how banking had overlooked the poor and was inspired by the earliest microfinance models, which lent money to low-income women and imparted them with skills, confidence, and community. One of the most inspiring of these was the Self-Employed Women's Association (SEWA) in India, a trade union for ragpickers, brick crushers, women who carry huge loads on their heads, and the like. Based on an ethos of strength in unity and a pro-poor philosophy, SEWA has grown to more than two million members. Though the women of SEWA may have limited material assets to claim for themselves, their union membership is their bond to one another, and it is upon this bond that SEWA extends microloans to them.

In 2015, on a cold and bitter January day in New Delhi, I

met Deepa Roy and Shruti Gonsalves, two of SEWA's directors, to travel with them on a visit to Acumen's new investee,
SEWA Grih Rin, a housing finance subsidiary that provides
loans to women who lack legal title to their land and thus are
unable to obtain mortgages to improve their homes.

Together, we drove more than two hours on crisscross-
ing highways whose twists and turns made me nauseated at
times. As we traveled farther from the city, the spaghetti roads
relaxed and narrowed, carrying us past farm fields and barren
industrial areas, until we reached Savda Ghevra, a massive
resettlement project for people rendered homeless by slum
clearances undertaken mainly by the Indian government to
remake parts of Delhi for major events such as the Com-
monwealth Games. Even before we reached our destination,
I couldn't help but imagine the four- to five-hour round-trip
bus commute people living in the area endured daily to look
for work in the city.

The unpaved settlement lanes were lined with a mix of
brick and poured-concrete houses painted Candy Land colors, as well as temporary shacks patched with bamboo poles,
sheets of plastic, cardboard boxes, and random pieces of fabric.
Soon we arrived at a two-story structure painted a startling
aqua green with a narrow, banister-free exterior staircase zig-
zagging sideways along the wall from ground level to a door on
the second floor. A diminutive woman with salt-and-pepper
hair fastened in a neat bun waited for us in the second-floor
doorway wearing socks and sandals and a mauve kurta layered
over a burgundy sweater and loose homespun shawl. A cataract clouded one of her bright eyes.

"My name is Dhanpati," the woman said, inviting us into
her small, clean, unheated home with pink interior walls. We
settled into white plastic chairs for what would be a three-hour

conversation. Dhanpati began by telling us about her "happy life" in the slums near Connaught Place, in Central Delhi, where she'd grown up knowing everyone and was confident she belonged. Describing the slum clearance that changed her life in 2008, she began to weep. "It was raining the day they came to evict us," she said.

The bulldozers knocked over her house and the dwellings of her longtime neighbors as if the structures were made of cardboard. The destruction became a harrowing storm of concrete and dirt, a lamentation of photographs, papers, and other mementos that churned and settled in the dust, all that remained of a once-vibrant community where she and her family lived and worked and dreamed.

Dhanpati's voice dropped to a whisper. "We were promised an allotment for land, but you had to pay seven thousand rupees [about a hundred dollars] to process the allotment, and most of us didn't have that kind of money. So, we lost everything."

For six years, Dhanpati's family of ten lived in a tent in a mustard field. "At least," she said, "we were close to the resettlement area and did our best to navigate the system, even if so little of the system actually worked." In the meantime, while her family was seeking some sort of assistance, Dhanpati began working at the supposedly free public toilet in the area. "Since government does not show up," she said, "I clean the toilet and charge people per use. They are happy I am there. Otherwise, it would be too filthy."

The opposite of accompaniment is separation. To enable the violence of slum clearances and other systems that strip people of life's possibilities requires a separation among and within ourselves. We reduce people to statistics in ways that dehumanizes them, keeping ourselves at a distance from the ugly realities of our decisions—or our inaction. We tell ourselves there is nothing else to be done. We blame victims' hardships on "the system" or characterize the poor as being unwilling or unworthy. We prefer not to know.

Thus does separation lie at the core of poverty. When policy makers decided to build a stadium in that Delhi slum, Dhanpati lost the only home she'd ever known. She felt humiliation in her homelessness, and shame in her inability to afford school for her children or find adequate health care. She bore the cost of too many cold and sleepless nights, accustomed to the loneliness that comes from feeling forever on the outside looking in, far away from her community. As Dhanpati told her story, her eyes flickered with both fight and desolation.

The separation that divides human beings also creates divisions within people, making them feel that they are less than others, that they are not worthy, that they are not enough. In reconnecting and reconstituting our common bonds, in accompanying one another, we have the greatest chance for renewal in our work, in our communities, and also within ourselves.

I asked Dhanpati if she trusted anyone.

"I trust only myself."

"What about SEWA?" I asked.

She smiled and said, "Yes. I trust them."

I asked why.

She looked around the room. "The people from SEWA visit," she said. "They fulfill promises. They lent me the money to build my home. They call me by my name. It is the only place in my life where I hear my name aloud. I am Dhanpati when they come."

I asked her to say more.

"Women like me lose our identity as soon as we marry. We are called wife or daughter-in-law or mother, but never our real names. SEWA makes me feel more important, as if I am somebody. I am Dhanpati. My name means 'Lord of Wealth.' I am somebody." Then she added proudly that she was current on her loan payments.

SEWA accompanies its female members, trains them with skills, and holds their hands when needed. At the same time, SEWA Grih Rin understands that it cannot and must not simply solve their members' problems, but must enable the women to solve problems for themselves. In turn, the women show up for one another.

SEWA Grih Rin's accompaniment of these women signals the union's fight for the rights of the self-employed, the land-less, and those who would change their own lives if given the chance and skills. The female members know that the institution is there to support them.

Accompaniment is a way of upholding your commitment to another's success. After her year as an Acumen fellow with a Rwandan coffee company that purchased beans from some of the poorest farmers on the planet, Australian-born Ramya Waran accepted a full-time job with the company, running operations while the CEO negotiated contracts with specialty buyers and maintained a more external presence. Ramya loved working with the farmers, and took great pride in being a female leader who supported women to lead themselves.

Sadly, that coffee company ultimately failed. While investors, including Acumen, focused on what it would mean to shut it down and do what was necessary to repay its creditors, Ramya turned her attention to the three hundred small-holder farmers who had lost their livelihoods. Despite her own exhaustion and working without a paycheck for months,

Ramya stayed on the job until every farmer felt secure and connected to a new company.

I will never forget my phone conversation with her. I was walking down a blustery New York City street while Ramya was up late in Kigali. "While the company is operational," she told me, "the best thing I can do for investors is to ensure a fair and profitable company. But with investors out and the company shutting down," she continued, "I have to focus on the farmers. Isn't that what we mean when we commit to standing with the poor? The bankruptcy wasn't their fault. They are the most vulnerable stakeholders of all here."

When faced with excruciating decisions involving divergent stakeholders, I call to mind and am inspired by Ramya's fierce determination to accompany the farmers. She had no financial cushion, and she was living in a foreign country, yet not for a minute did she allow the situation to be about her. Ramya was there to accompany the farmers, to stand with the poor so they could carry on with their prospects intact after the company that had trained and supported them collapsed.

In times of both success and failure, we can choose with whom we stand. Going beyond yourself to enable others not just to persevere but to thrive lies at the heart of accompaniment. Twenty-first-century capitalism rewards money, power, and fame, not the immeasurable impact we have on a person's confidence, their courage, or their ability to, say, remain in school or even to make it through another day. This failure to recognize important work imperils us all.

By rewarding only what we can measure, we perpetuate systems that fail to honor that which we value most—and the price we pay is nothing less than our collective soul. But we can choose to build new systems grounded in a moral framework premised on the belief that we are here on earth to serve others and to sustain our planet for the next generation. That starts with the simple, dedicated act of accompanying one another.

At a time when elements of the developed and the developing world exist within every country, the principle of accompaniment is universally relevant. As countries become wealthier and more unequal, they inevitably become more individualistic and fearful, breeding grounds for isolation, loneliness, and mistrust.

Many models of accompaniment in the developing world are based on the understanding that people yearn to belong, to be cared for, and that individual communities thrive when they are parts of larger communities. In other words, human beings thrive when we believe someone cares about us. It isn't much more complicated than that.

During the HIV/AIDS crisis in Africa, many organizations employed a community health worker (CHW) model, enlisting and transforming ordinary community members into health workers who accompanied their neighbors. The CHWs would show up at the homes of HIV-infected patients to make sure they were eating correctly and taking their medicines. The best of these health workers emotionally accompanied the ill, making them feel seen and worthy. In turn, the CHWs become valued members and leaders of society.

Manmeet Kaur, an American daughter of South Asian immigrants, worked both in South Africa and India, where she experienced the CHW model firsthand before returning to New York to pursue her MBA. In 2013, she founded a company in Manhattan's Harlem neighborhood called City Health Works, which aims to integrate CHWs and coaches into the U.S. health care system. She'd seen unskilled South African women receive a few months' training and then support patients with HIV, often with remarkable results. "Why couldn't residents serve as peer counselors in the States?" she wondered.

In Harlem, as in much of the United States, significant numbers of residents suffer from chronic diseases such as diabetes, asthma, and hypertension. Manmeet reasoned that partnering directly with these patients could help them modify their lifestyles and provide companionship while also saving the government and insurance companies a considerable amount of money.

On another wintry January day, this time in 2017, I went to City Health Works to visit a local health coach named Destini Belton, an African American whose uncluttered attire (black pants, a red sweater, and stud earrings) and pulled-back hair were paired with a straightforward personality. Personable, smart, and matter-of-fact, Destini spoke to me as if we were old friends while we walked to a colorful community center in Spanish Harlem. Inside the center, we passed a gym full of young boys playing basketball, and then a dance hall where older men and women were dancing salsa, finally to arrive at a room filled with thirty women and three or four men playing cards or bingo or mah-jongg. A petite elderly Chinese woman walked from table to table offering oranges and powdery cookies.

We joined a group of black and Latina women who were gladdened to see Destini and who welcomed me warmly. We talked about their lives and what it felt like to be clients of City Health Works. Maria, wearing a wool cap and holding a cane, spoke about how much she loved feeling part of something. "Destini takes me to the grocery store and teaches me how to shop for healthy foods," she said. "I appreciate that. These people know what they're doing. We go on walks, and Destini checks in on me to see that I'm taking the right meds. When-ever I have a problem, I just call her." As Maria spoke, the other women at the table nodded their heads in agreement.

"But are you healthier?" I asked.

"You bet I'm healthier!" Maria exclaimed. "I've lost weight and I feel good. It's been a long time since I had to go to the hospital."

I turned to Destini and asked for her reaction to so many compliments.

"It does make me feel valued," she responded. "I had a dead-end job before this one, just working in retail. But now I'm being trained. I'm contributing to the community and my family."

I asked Destini what she appreciated most about her job as a health coach.

"I teach the women how to do better at eating and shop-ping," she said. "And they appreciate it. Some have a better sense of hope now. They've been suffering from the same dis-eases for so many years, and now they are seeing for the first time that they can feel better if they manage their issues."

"Has seeing the women changed you?" I asked.

"I feel more important now, and my own eating also has improved."

"Why do you think your eating habits have changed?"

"If you're the coach, you'd better practice what you preach!" Destini responded. "Being a coach is helping more than my patients. It's helping my whole family and some of my friends, too." I realized as she spoke that in teaching one family member how to take better care of their health, Destini was impacting extended families, including her own.

As Manmeet later explained, "We teach our health coaches to start by asking three questions of their clients: What are your fears? What are you struggling with? What motivates you to live a longer life? After a couple of visits, clients might disclose more sensitive struggles that are contributing to their poor health, whether they fear taking their medicines or are too ashamed to go to local food pantries. The health coaches learn to listen, and the clients feel seen, because our coaches have similar life experiences. People from vulnerable situations are not just defined by their situations. They have individual and collective strengths."

As for the health workers, Manmeet added, some have told her that they observe themselves "leveling up," acquiring new skills and believing more deeply in themselves because the company assumes they can do more than they imagined for themselves.

City Health Works now has accompanied more than two thousand clients in Harlem and is taking the model to other parts of New York City. Manmeet has proven that the model lowers overall health costs, securing state contracts that will allow her to build a profitable company.

People sometimes ask how "accompaniment" scales as a principle. I would say that how we support one another is an ethos, a way of seeing others—and ourselves. If we spread that ethos, and if we celebrate those who do it well, then accompaniments and the benefits from them will only increase.

Accompaniment is not only for a business or an organization. It is a framework for a more inclusive, caring society. Wherever people feel lonely, isolated, or anxious, there is an opportunity: to prevent chronic disease, to support the elderly, to take care of the very young, to help the sick and suffering, to help prisoners feel less alone, and to enable the formerly incarcerated and drug users to get back on their feet. All of us will at some point need to be accompanied. All of us have the power to accompany someone else in need.

At the end of my day in Harlem, I reflected on its connection to that chilly visit to Dhanpati's pink house on the other side of the world. I was mesmerized by her story: Dhanpati's was a narrative of an entire system that people like her across the world are expected to navigate though every card in the deck is stacked against them.

That day, Dhanpati noticed that I'd not stopped shivering from the freezing air since we'd arrived. She offered us hot tea and biscuits. We declined, knowing the family would have to cross the street to buy water and milk for the tea. But Dhanpati would not accept my refusal.

"If I visit you, you will give me tea. Now you are visiting my home. I will do the same."

I accepted the milky sweet tea gratefully, delighting in the shot of sugar and heat. Dhanpati instantly offered me a second cup. My desire to take it was slowed only by my sense of shame. By now, the entire family had joined our conversation and was waiting patiently for us to be sated before they served themselves.

The irony of Dhanpati's attentiveness and her focus on service—her accompaniment—was not lost on me. Who was the real giver here? In that tiny teacup was an ocean of grace provoking me to examine how often I failed to pause and notice the needs of those right in front of me. I had much to learn from Dhanpati, and from the way SEWA Grih Rin accompanied her so that she could accompany others.

This is the secret of accompaniment: I will hold a mirror to you and show you your value, bear witness to your suffering and to your light. And over time, you will do the same for me, for within the relationship lies the promise of our shared dignity and the mutual encouragement needed to do the hard things.

Whatever you aim to do, whatever problem you hope to address, remember to accompany those who are struggling, who are left out, who lack the capabilities needed to solve their own problems. We are each other's destiny. Beneath the hard skills and firm strategic priorities needed to resolve our greatest challenges lies the soft, fertile ground of our shared humanity. In that place of hard and soft is sustenance enough to nourish the entire human family.

Chapter 12

TELL STORIES
THAT MATTER

"Aren't you too old to be so idealistic about Africa?" a prominent Nigerian businessman taunted me with a smile during a
2009 dinner party in a posh home in Accra, Ghana. Around
the long rectangular table with me were eighteen West African
businessmen and my colleague Catherine Casey Nanda. The
air held the scent of frangipani and formality.

Catherine and I were at that table to introduce Acumen to
potential philanthropic supporters in West Africa, to paint a
picture of what Acumen was capable of igniting in the region,
and to set the stage for raising local funds. Catherine had
already shared anecdotes of potential investments we would
make in Nigeria and Ghana, stories that offered strong testimony to the potential of our work. The night had been pro-
gressing swimmingly.

Then I launched into a perhaps too-rhapsodic address about
Acumen's work from a more global perspective. The man's
question about my idealism took me by surprise. His words
were skeptical; his tone, cynical. I was conscious of my race,
my outsider status, and the larger stakes of this first meeting to

introduce Acumen to West Africa. At the same time, I experienced the man's provocation as an affront to what my team and our collective work represented. Into the center of that table, with its starched and pressed linen and its sterling silver, attended by uniformed men wearing pristine white gloves, the charismatic questioner had thrown down a gauntlet.

I reached across the finery to accept the challenge, asking the man what he meant by his question.

"Just what I said," he responded flatly. "Aren't you too old to be so idealistic about Africa?"

Now all eyes were on me.

"I choose idealism as an antidote to cynicism," I said, locking the man's eyes with my own. "That doesn't mean I don't see the ugly or the challenges. I'm trying to picture how I would inspire an audience by describing only the continent's underbelly. Isn't West Africa much more than that?"

Internally, I could feel the presence of two voices, one telling me to put a muzzle on my mouth; the other one urging me forward. "Would you rather I spoke about some of my experiences with incompetence or corruption or abject indifference?" I asked, as the timbre of my voice gradually crescendoed. "For I could give a lecture on any of those topics. I could also share anecdotes of elites who talk a big game of love and peace only to let down their countrymen and women, knowing that as long as they are in the 'right clubs,' the world will applaud their riches and ignore their misdeeds. Or I could recount times I've been held up, mugged, assaulted, robbed, and threatened. I could speak about colleagues of mine who fought for justice, for *years*, only to be murdered during the Rwandan genocide; or describe others who capitulated finally to their insecurities and their thirst for power, ultimately joining the perpetrators of that bloodbath."

I took a breath, if only to stem my swelling emotions. "Sometimes," I concluded, "there are days when I have to fight a hardening of my own soul from seeing too many people treated like throwaways. So, yes, I can paint the opposite of idealistic for you. But as the Nigerian author Chimamanda Adichie says, there is more than a single story."

Of course, I can tell stories of lightness and darkness about *every* country I know, especially about my own nation. But we were talking about a continent that had shaped my identity and, in many ways, had taught me what real love is. Anger rose inside my chest like a clenched fist as that part of me that had committed to showing up with real love, not easy love, felt threatened.

And the man had questioned me on the wrong night.

Or maybe it was the right one.

I was in the middle of a family crisis that seemed to parallel our dinner discussion. A month earlier, my thirty-five-year-old sister, Amy, had undergone brain surgery that had left her entire left side paralyzed. The surgeons had told her she might never walk again. She was in rehab in New York City, and we knew, regardless of the outcome, that the road ahead would be a long one.

But you don't want to mess with my sister. Amy understood the prognosis; we all did. She knew that parts of her body would be slower to return to mobility, if they ever did, and that other parts held more potential. She was studying every kind of therapy imaginable, supported by a tight community of family and friends who accompanied her, aware that in the end, she was the one who would have to do the excruciating work of recovery. And my sister kept to a single narrative: You don't get to choose what happens to you. But you do get to choose how you respond.

"When I'm in the room with my sister," I said to those at

the table, "we listen carefully to the surgeon's dreary words, but we don't dwell on them; instead, we talk about the wedding my sister Amy is planning with her prince of a fiancé. I tell her how much I'm looking forward to dancing with her."

I continued: "Some might say that is foolish optimism—or too *idealistic*, but I believe you become the story you choose to tell. While my family can accompany my sister, that's all we can do. Amy has to do the heroic work of fighting every day. She is focused and tough. And she refuses to acquiesce to narratives that would have her accept what many see as inevitable.

"And you know what?" I continued. "Mark my words: I will dance with my sister at her wedding."

I paused long enough to notice that everyone had stopped eating.

"Make of it what you'd like, but I am dedicated to contributing to the growing movement of enterprising, committed, capable, ethical, and public-spirited African social entrepreneurs who are serving their communities, nations, and this very continent. I am betting on individuals who will not be hemmed in by other people's narratives.

"Look, the negatives I described about Africa are truths, just like those that my sister's surgeons hold about probabilities of recovery. Equally as real, however, are the stories of astonishing creativity and hard work on this continent. Kenya's mobile banking technologies have leapfrogged services in the West. Nigeria's Nollywood is the third-largest film industry in the world. I've met brilliant scientists, technologists, doctors, musicians, poets, writers, philanthropists, activists, teachers, and, yes, even politicians here, all of whom are focused on serving the greater good. I have been humbled by the wisdom of people in this region who've known great suffering yet still are determined to try to give and to forgive.

"It is all here. All of it. The question is which stories will we tell, those reeking of despair or those imbued with a hard-edged hope."

The man's mouth broke into a toothy smile. "Hey," he said, "I'm a journalist. I'm paid to be skeptical."

"I get that," I replied. "I just have to beat the drum for hope, you know, as a radical response to cynicism."

He insisted he wasn't cynical, just skeptical, and everyone laughed. Maybe because the discussion was so real and so raw, Catherine and I found ardent supporters that night, people whose efforts helped us build a program, now based in Lagos, Nigeria, whose stories of possibility Acumen and scores of fellows and entrepreneurs can now tell.

The job of the moral leader—which is the job of *all of us*—is to learn to tell the stories that matter, stories that unite and inspire, reinforcing our individual and collective potential, and paint a picture of the future that we can build and inhabit together. Stories that matter are *not* stories that demean, deride, divide, ridicule, belittle, blame, or shame. We must take the harder path of telling stories that hold our truths, both the ugly and the beautiful, while remaining laser-focused on the possible.

Stories matter, for they have consequences. The stories we choose to tell often define who we become. Indeed, recent advances in science are proving that the narratives we tell about ourselves and others influence even our health and longevity. Show me a happy person, and I will show you someone who owns her own narrative, who shares most happenings in positive ways and tragic events as turning points rather than end points.

In consciously shaping our personal narratives, we find the freedom to become our best selves, and can do more to accompany and inspire others. Take the case of Teresa Njoroge. An elegant young Kenyan woman with a successful career in banking, in January 2011 she was jailed, along with her three-month-old daughter, in the Langata Women Maximum Security Prison in Nairobi, Kenya, for a crime she didn't commit—for a year. Teresa could have told a story of being a victim, a story of bitterness, rage, or revenge. Instead, she claimed a more positive narrative for herself, turning a tragic and costly miscarriage of justice into a springboard for service and possibility—and without letting the broken criminal justice system off the hook.

Teresa shared the story of her arrest during one of my Nairobi visits in 2017. "I loved my career and everything that went with it, especially the status and prestige," she said. "But then I handled a fraudulent transaction unknowingly. The police arrested and charged me with fraud, and that same arresting officer told me that if I paid him ten thousand dollars, the case would disappear.

"Even if I had the money," Teresa continued, "why would I pay a bribe when I had done nothing wrong? I spent the next two and a half years in and out of courts, fighting to prove my innocence. It was humiliating to see my face and name in newspapers and on television. And then, just before the court date, the court offered me the chance for freedom—*if I paid fifty thousand dollars*. But the investigation had produced no evidence whatsoever of any crime, so I had no fear of conviction. I refused to pay, and I found myself locked behind a prison gate."

The prison guard in Langata issued Teresa a number as a proxy for her name. As a prisoner, she was given a loose-fitting black-and-white-striped cotton uniform to wear just like everyone else. Though her first days in the prison were full of trepidation, Teresa quickly came to understand how many of her fellow inmates had simply fallen through the cracks of society, ending up in jail after having been falsely convicted, or used as a scapegoat in corrupt systems where the poor and most vulnerable bear the brunt of society's failures.

Living as a prisoner, among prisoners, Teresa came to reinterpret the misguided stories we tell ourselves about those who are incarcerated. "Too often, we criminalize poverty," she said. "Poor women are arrested for lacking licenses to hawk their wares on the streets. Technically, they are breaking the law, but they are trying to sell what little they have so that they can survive. The same applies when mothers sometimes steal tiny portions of food to feed their children or find medicines to keep a sick relative alive. Again, they might be guilty, but aren't their stories more about broken health systems, broken education systems, broken economic systems? Don't those stories matter more than the individual infringements of women and men cast aside by society before they even had a real chance to participate?"

Teresa resolved to work on the challenges of the criminal justice system. "My time in prison was a blessing in disguise," she reflected.

Upon her release, she founded an NGO called Clean Start, to help female prisoners gain the skills and confidence to participate as full citizens of society. This mission has become part of who she is: "Daily, I think about the women in prison and those who have left but are kept out of society's opportunities. Daily, I wonder how their children are faring."

Teresa's story begins with the narrative that matters most to her—her own. The truer we are to the details of our inner and outer lives, the more universal those details become. In time, Teresa's story has become the story of *all* imprisoned people. By hewing to her own deepest realities, she has been able to extend empathy toward prisoners as a collective group and acknowledge that she is in them, and they, in her.

The moral leader elevates, providing pathways to redemption and meaning. Teresa's narrative is not just about enduring hardship. It is also about second chances, and taking charge of your own life. She now enters jails willingly, lovingly, and finds in the female inmates a life force that enlivens her spirit and fortifies her will.

The psychiatrist and Holocaust survivor Viktor Frankl wrote, "Between stimulus and response there is a space. In that space is our power to choose our response. In our response lies our growth and our freedom." The narratives we choose to tell ourselves and others can be extremely consequential, steering us toward roads of despair or pathways to freedom. The choice is ours to make.

Of course, the space "between stimulus and response" is no space at all for those who respond emotionally or defensively to every Facebook post or tweet. Social media encourages us to post fabulous stories and images, to curate our personal "brands" based on "best of" lives lived externally. Meanwhile, our internal realities may painfully diverge in comparison, making it even more challenging than in previous generations to be honest with ourselves about who we are and who we want to be. But the ability to tell stories that matter starts with the story of self. Those narratives must be truthful and vulnerable, and grounded in self-awareness, if we hope to engender trust and enable self-discovery in those around us.

We fail in this accounting if we reduce our own narrative to a single defining story. I've known too many people who cling to a narrow definition of themselves, repeating the same story so many times that they divorce themselves from their own words, thereby limiting their potential for growth. I once knew a man who started every introduction recounting his youth, how he would lie on a mat beneath a yellow moon, his belly empty and aching as his mother pretended to cook over an open fire while, in reality, stirring nothing but water. He shared this narrative in ways that captivated every audience—at least, the first few times they heard it.

Over time, I realized that my friend used his childhood story less to teach or illuminate than to protect from rejection of the man he had become. While that impoverished boy would always be a part of him, he had since become a privileged adult with significant opportunities and responsibilities. By failing to integrate his new story into the old, he neither made peace with that frightened, hungry little boy nor fully acknowledged his older, successful, complicated self. Consequently, everyone was cheated from knowing the fullness of him in the present; and *he* lost most of all.

In that same vein, diminishing ourselves to elicit sympathy or pity from those more powerful than ourselves might result in short-term material payoffs; but those narratives risk reinforcing negative biases and spiritual depletion. I once visited a private school for underprivileged but talented youth in East Africa, and I was overjoyed by the quality of the young people I met there. At the same time, I became increasingly dismayed at the way each of them introduced him- or herself. A beautiful fourteen-year-old girl with a veil draped softly over her head shared her name and then immediately launched into her story as a poor village girl who was beaten by her recently deceased father. A few minutes later, I met a fifteen-year-old boy dressed in a perfectly pressed school uniform, his hair neatly combed. He shook my hand professionally. Before I could ask a question, he told me that his parents were poor and had no means to educate him. A third and then a fourth youngster handed me similar stories of suffering.

My head in a whirl, I thanked the young people for their time, then excused myself to seek out the headmaster. I found him outside the school's well-stocked music room—a tall, balding man in a blue suit. "Your students are remarkable," I began. "I could imagine each of them running a company, a school system, or even a country in their lifetimes. But I also feel uncomfortable with the way they introduce themselves. Rather than painting pictures of endless, hopeless poverty, why can't they present themselves as the highly talented students they are, young future-oriented people who have earned a right to attend any school on earth and succeed?"

The headmaster spoke plainly and slowly. "Most visitors, especially donors, want to know that we use their money for poor children who would not have the opportunity for education without them. Philanthropists want to feel good about their giving; we are simply helping them do that. Without their funds, there would be no school."

"But what about the young people themselves?" I asked. "Doesn't this beggar approach lock them into presenting themselves as poor and grateful, rather than talented and brimming with potential? What message does this send to the students? And doesn't it reinforce the savior complex in wealthy individuals?"

The headmaster's expression was a mix of understanding and irritation. "It is hard to raise money," he said, and sighed.

I agreed with the hard part, though I deplored his methods. We will not build strong institutions or confident, capable people if we don't tell the whole truth. And we diminish ourselves when we tell—or heed—stories that reinforce negative stereotypes.

On the other hand, if we spin yarns from hyperbole and empty promises, we feel like frauds. I was lucky to be raised by a mythmaking mother who infused her children with the belief that we could be anything we wanted to be, provided we worked hard and didn't quit. And I was regularly cut down to size by a rowdy bunch of siblings who, even today, remind me of the foibles of my youth, making it impossible for me to take myself too seriously. Stories shape and then reshape each of us. Stories matter.

Too many children are raised on narratives that reinforce a sense of inferiority or meekness. Some of those children grow into adults who never escape society's low expectations. Others seem imprisoned in bitter allegories of their own making. Somewhere along the way, they forgot that our stories are not set in stone. We might inherit stories, but it is up to us to craft the narratives of our lives, just as Teresa, the falsely accused banker, did.

We are raised on stories about characters in bedtime fables, proverbs, religious texts, and family anecdotes; these shape our worldviews and color our moral frameworks. Many of the narratives we inherit also demean other people. Think of Vimal, the Acumen fellow who, as a boy, was repeatedly told myths about his caste, deemed the lowliest of people, humans who deserved no livelihood other than cleaning toilets or removing human waste. That story was a "fiction," if you will, to borrow a meaning for that word from the Israeli philosopher Yuval Harari. For what is caste if not a story written by a group of people long ago to explain the world to themselves (and others) in ways that protected their privilege by making others inferior and giving a false sense of order to society?

Our most inspirational leaders share stories of human possibility in which we can see ourselves; consider the speeches of Mahatma Gandhi, Martin Luther King Jr., and Nelson Mandela, for example. Creating counternarratives that refuse to divide and diminish requires a reclamation of the parables and histories of people too often unheard, eliciting from them insightful, true stories that resonate with everyone's humanity. Good news lies in spectacular role models of fortitude and forbearance, decency and dignity, models who exist in every hamlet and slum, in every city and on every isolated mountain.

Recounting tales of possibility also impacts the culture we create. If you want to inspire courageous acts of integrity, celebrate those who act with courage. As the philosopher Plato wrote, "What is honored in a country is cultivated there."

As the ambulance company Ziqitza began to expand across India (as told in chapter 10), the founders knew that the question of culture was paramount to their success. The company built its reputation on delivering effective services without bribery or corruption, and that demanded shifting the expectations not only of the private and public partners, but of the drivers, emergency medical technicians (EMTs), and patients as well.

The right stories reinforced those values.

"We are talking about people's lives," said Sumit Basu, the company's regional manager in Odisha. "What else matters when you have this responsibility?"

Sumit relayed the story of Pratap Kumar Sethi, an EMT who noticed an open wallet beside an unconscious man thrown from his vehicle during an accident. Pratap gathered up the wallet and found $350 in rupees, more than several months of his salary. He carried the wallet to the hospital, holding it tightly until the man involved in the accident was conscious enough to receive it.

At Ziqitza, Pratap's story was cause for celebration. The

company made him a hero, elevating him as a role model and getting local media to spread the news and reinforce the company's values. The drivers told me how proud they felt to be part of a company that was "good," and stressed that seeing Pratap celebrated publicly inspired them to do the right thing as well. Ziqitza cofounder Shaffi Mather later affirmed that a stronger culture translated into more effective results.

Our hope for a moral revolution rests on telling stories that unite, that challenge stereotypes and easy prejudices, and that ultimately reinforce our dignity. Telling those stories effectively, however, requires a humility that acknowledges the light and dark in all of us. When you dare to tell your full story, you will inevitably touch people who relate to your most vulnerable elements. And as you dive into the more painful stories from your past, you may find clues to help shape the story of who you want to become.

At Acumen, we ask new cohorts of fellows to do an exercise called River of Life. First, the fellows pair off and discuss the twists and turns of their lives; then each fellow shares his or her story with the full group (twenty or so people). Each narrative contains moments of success and joy, and inevitably times of sorrow or hurt, tragedy or shame—and sometimes all of these. They tell of childhoods trapped in crushing poverty, of tragic losses borne too young. They have grown up in refugee camps, or they have lived in terror of the Taliban, Naxalites, paramilitaries, or the police. They have been betrayed; they have been abandoned. Some have suffered physical or sexual abuse. The stories make you weep. Every fellow has a story worth telling, all of them adding to the story of us, a story still unfolding.

Listening to people share stories of trauma or loss within their life trajectories is a profound reminder that our tragedies neither define nor destroy us. How we *respond* to our trauma plays a much greater role; and therein lies the groundwork for the most important stories we can write, not with pen and paper but in the way we conduct our lives. The stories shared during the River of Life exercise are reminders that some individuals choose service and kindness or commit to fighting for justice in order to defy the darkness.

Shameem Akhtar was born to a thirteen-year-old father and a fifteen-year-old mother in a speck of a village outside a small city called Mirpur Khas, in the vast desert of Sindh, Pakistan. Shameem's father, just a boy himself, was initially devastated at bringing a girl into the world. The story for girls in his tribe was that of being unworthy, a burden. He and his wife wanted more for their child.

Shameem's father had an elder brother, one of the first in his family to attend university. The elder suggested that the young couple raise Shameem as a boy—dress her as a boy, treat her as a boy, and, most important, educate her as a boy. No girl of their village had ever attended school, and this plan would allow her to learn.

Thus began Shameem's adventures as a little boy, climbing trees, riding bicycles, and attending school. While her cousins stayed indoors learning to cook and clean, Shameem sat at the feet of elder men during *jurgas*, or councils, absorbing the rules and practices of political negotiations. Unlike the village girls, she had the chance to read newspapers, ask questions of male elders, and dream of other places.

During a long discussion with Shameem at Acumen's Karachi office in July 2018, she shared with me the contradictions of her childhood: "I felt sorry for the girls in my village but disliked spending time with them, for they spoke about clothing and makeup, things that bored me. It made no sense that the boys had the same hands and feet as I did, yet were treated so differently. I studied hard to be the best in my class and prove what girls could do."

I asked her if she had dreaded finally "becoming" a girl.

"Yes, very much," she admitted. "By the time I was sixteen, the villagers could see I was female, and many men insulted my father. Maybe they didn't like watching a daughter do better than their sons." And though being treated as a boy gave her physical and mental confidence, Shameem still feared walking alone in a dress at the university she was then attending.

And her story was not hers alone. Though her father was not yet thirty when Shameem left for university, he accompanied her through every challenge. When she expressed her apprehension to him, he said simply, "I didn't raise you to be afraid."

Though her father endured misunderstanding and ridicule for the way he raised Shameem, his determination that she succeed never wavered. This is a story of a father's love as well as of a daughter's courage and capability.

When we dare to push the edges of comfort, the narratives we tell ourselves can shape-shift and transform the world. After university, Shameem learned of a job opportunity with a regional NGO a five-hour bus ride away from her village. Again, she asked for her father's blessing; and again, he said yes. But she was the one who decided to live a story that would have no limits, regardless of the costs. Her education had gifted Shameem with dreams unavailable to "people like her," and she was not going to squander them.

Shameem's new job exposed her to her country's diverse people and places, and also to its poverty. "Now I could see how much more privileged I was than poor women who were dying in childbirth because they were too far from a hospital, or whose poverty forced them to choose which of their children to feed."

Her perspective broadened further when, as an Acumen fellow in 2015, she met with leaders from across her country.

In 2016, inspired by the life choices of others, Shameem decided to leave her job at the NGO and return to her region to bring education to other little girls. By then, parents of children were more amenable to the idea, especially those who had witnessed Shameem's family receive the money she sent back home. But nothing prepared her for the feeling of "seeing a classroom full of little Shameems" looking back at her as she told the stories of Nelson Mandela and other history-making individuals. Those bright, shining faces were worth the cost of her two-hour bus ride, twice daily, to reach the schools. In the course of the next few years, Shameem would also earn her PhD.

Shameem's narrative is filled with layers and lessons—about the value of education, the power of courage, and the strength that comes from having someone in your court. Her story also reveals the incalculable potential lost when we deny any human being the freedom to learn and contribute.

And Shameem does not need anyone else to tell her story. In November 2017, I had the great privilege of curating a session for the TEDWomen conference in New Orleans, a session in which Shameem participated. She arrived from Karachi on Halloween night, and the city streets were overflowing with residents in outlandish costumes, portraying every ghoulish, irreverent celebrity character and personality imaginable. Shameem took it all in stride, though I assured her that Halloween in New Orleans was not the only story of that city.

Two days later, she stood proudly onstage. The TED conference had given this child of the desert, born to illiterate teenage parents, a platform to speak in her own words, on her own behalf. In return, Shameem spoke for every child who has been overlooked because of their gender, race, ethnicity, class, or disability.

Our collective story is a mosaic of narratives that inspire our better selves, counter those who would divide us, and reveal the hidden gifts and capacities that the world would rather not see. The story of us is ultimately that of love forever unfolding. And no story matters more than that.

One more thing: one of the most indelible memories of my life is dancing wildly with my sister, Amy, at her epic, unforgettable wedding.

Chapter 13

EMBRACE THE
BEAUTIFUL STRUGGLE

In November 1992, several friends and I trekked the Borneo rainforest accompanied by two hardy guides, Mustafa and Gun. We were there to explore the forest ecosystem, natural and human. The trip was rough going at times; we trudged for weeks along narrow pathways through dense, unforgiving vegetation. We would have been wearied by the intense humidity that kept our clothing perpetually damp had a constant flow of leeches not jumped onto our limbs and distracted us with more pressing concerns. At night, random bugs and enormous beetles had a way of crawling into our sleeping bags. Our fresh food ran out after a few days, leaving us with only heaping piles of rice and canned sardines for meals. Yet, we daily experienced wonder and were regularly astonished by the lushness of layered jungle terrain punctuated by shafts of sunlight peeking through the filigreed forest canopy overhead.

Our guides were delightful. Though their English was basic at best, Mustafa and Gun helped us witness firsthand the cost of human activity wrought by commercial logging, stopping to point toward groves of tree stumps and wide roads plunging violently into what used to be fertile forest. We didn't spot a single mammal on the journey, and heard just one gibbon call out to others. As for the local people, an "Indonesianization" policy had consigned nomadic tribes to reservation-like villages, uprooting them from their homes and denying them their culture.

In the course of our journey, I began to see more clearly the symbiotic relationship between human beings and the environment. Men hauled teak and other hardwoods from the rainforest to sell across the world, animals lost their habitat, and humans lost part of the world's lungs. Native peoples could not sustain themselves under the onslaught, and the entire world paid a price. Here, at the source of our shared ecosystem, the violence of poverty and greed were palpable.

Both guides seemed to sense when I was feeling nearly overwhelmed by the destruction wrought by human beings' thirst for things. In those moments, the guides would attempt to distract me from my ruminations, directing my attention to an exotic orchid or tangled vines or moon shadows dancing across the trunks of skinny trees shimmying in the night breeze. I'd find in the astonishing beauty around me a sign of life urging itself to survive. I'd also hear an admonition of what we would lose if we didn't repair the world.

On one of our final nights in the rainforest, the Borneo journey gifted the group a moment of transcendence. At the end of a long, sweltering day, we rested in a small clearing. We were all bone-tired, unrestored by the sticky sponge baths we'd taken in a nearby blackwater creek. We ate what we could of our regular canned dinner and then sat silently with our guides beneath a veil of mosquito netting. Knowing we were nearing the end of our adventure, I was desperate to convey my gratitude and admiration to the guides.

With no knowledge of Bahasa, the guides' language, I could express only rudimentary thoughts through my words. But if we lacked a common language, I reasoned, maybe there were songs we shared. I started to sing, hoping I'd hit a tune the guides would recognize. After trying and failing with at least a dozen songs, I finally chanced upon one of my favorite Christmas carols: "Silent night, holy night, / All is calm, all is bright . . ."

Upon hearing the familiar tune, Mustafa and Gun both smiled and began to sing. The others joined in, and our little group became a choir, harmonizing in four languages: English, Bahasa, German, and French. I felt myself extended not only to my fellow journeyers but to the forest around us and all its living things. Long, arduous days immersed in nature had stripped us of artifice, granting us access to a deeper level of "knowing" somehow. The night's flickering lights and unbidden symphony illuminated the possible, expanding my soul's longing to know that all could be healed.

Silent night, holy night.

When we finally could sing no more, the six of us held hands for a moment and bowed to the divinity we experienced in one another.

That night, I went to sleep full of awe and secure in my belief of an illimitable consciousness that binds us with all living things. I silently recommitted to work toward human dignity and a more sustainable earth. And I understood then that skills and resources are not enough to solve our problems: we must ground our systems in a spiritual foundation big enough to sustain our astonishing diversity. Such a foundation is based on the notion of transcendence, that all living things are interconnected, that we are deserving of dignity.

Humans' growing awareness of our interdependence is

driving people across the planet to reimagine and try to live by a new set of guiding principles. I see this in the growing army of social entrepreneurs across the globe, including those you've met in these pages. Some are devoted to expanding human possibilities. Others are fighting to save the planet, to reverse the march of so many species toward extinction, to temper the destructive elements of technology. No matter your field, there is much to learn from activists imagining and building new systems together for our twenty-first-century world.

For example, environmental and animal rights activists are pressing, sometimes successfully, to enshrine "nonhuman rights." In Colombia in April 2018, a group of twenty-five young people won a court ruling to "recognize the Colombian Amazon as an entity, subject of rights, and beneficiary of the protection, conservation, maintenance and restoration." New Zealand and several U.S. states have won similar cases.

This was a game changer based on a moral framework: if corporations are, for legal purposes, given "personhood," and if rivers and forests can have rights, so might animals. Groups across the globe are beginning to argue that some mammals like chimpanzees, elephants, and orcas should be assigned certain rights to protect their survival. These new frameworks are manifestations of the belief that we can, and must, transcend our individual needs and desires to build structures that work for and sustain all of us.

More than a quarter century since that night in the Borneo rainforest, my youthful aspirations feel affirmed when I see the progress we are making in reimagining a new economic system that is both inclusive and sustainable. Yet, I'm bemused when young people earnestly ask me how I can be so old and still so passionate about my commitment to work toward dignity, despite all the inevitable setbacks and failures.

I feel a growing sense of urgency to do more in the decades that lie in front of me. All of us know that the work of change is hard, that it is long—sometimes decades long, sometimes lifetimes long.

So, how do any of us sustain? Every change agent must find within herself the strength to carry on through the dark times and the courage to push against a resistant status quo, not just for a couple of years but, potentially, for decades. Anger can go a long way, yet it eventually whittles the soul. External awards may be reinforcing, yet whatever comfort they provide is fleeting. Any honor bestowed by others can be taken away. There must be something more, something that nourishes the spirit and makes slogging for years through the mud and grime of social change bearable.

I have found sustenance in a part of the journey that few talked about when I began: beauty. To paraphrase Dr. King, there is beauty in struggle. There is beauty around us, beacons of the possible, especially if we still ourselves long enough to recognize it. Beauty inspires and motivates. Beauty sustains. The key for each of us is to define what beauty means for us, to think of it not as superfluous or indulgent but as an essential part of what it means to be human.

Life is hard—which may be why humans have insisted on creating beauty in even the darkest times and in the meanest places. In every poor community I've ever visited, beauty manifests. Think of tribes the world over that embellish bowls and farm implements or weave evocative imagery into everyday fabrics. In the harsh climes of India's and Pakistan's deserts, women collect water wearing the brightest colors imaginable, multiple clay pots stacked on their heads and steadied with confident arms encircled with sparkly bangles. In war zones, I've witnessed little girls walking down dangerous streets in pretty white party dresses. Even in the grimmest slums of Kampala or Lagos, women hang beautifully embroidered, diaphanous curtains to cover walls made of corrugated tin patched with cardboard and coffee cans: beauty for survival, for bringing life itself to parched and tired places.

Beauty is an expression of human dignity. It resides in the work of showing up, of extending ourselves and bringing kindness when we feel like being anything but kind. Beauty lives in the narratives of those who are striving to overcome profound obstacles just to survive. It thrives in the bonds of human connection and the quiet moments of contemplative reflection. Let beauty be a powerful touchstone, not only to reinforce your own resolve, but to rejuvenate those you serve.

The practice of paying attention is a form of beauty, a kind of prayer, connecting us in ways that elevate. Hone that skill so you can encourage it in others. In the 1990s, I volunteered at Phoenix House, a drug rehabilitation center on the Upper West Side of New York City. My job was simply to talk to the female clients. Unsure of how to break the ice and move to deeper topics, I thought I'd try prompting conversation with a poem, and chose Maya Angelou's "Phenomenal Woman." I suggested we go around the room, each of us reading one line, thereby linking ourselves with a daisy chain of words.

As we started to take turns reading, it became clear that some of the women were functionally illiterate. As I listened to one woman stumble over the first word in the poem—"Pretty women . . ."—I felt ashamed that I'd set them up for failure.

Then something magical happened.

The woman sounded out, "Pret-ty" and then reached toward the group as if to grab the second word.

The other women, in turn, leaned toward her, their mouths forming the "wo" sound in "women," lips puckered as if to blow her a kiss. Soon they were a unified voice, quietly urging, cheering at the end of each line. By the last stanza, we were a chorus, a proud group of women singing from the rooftops: "'Cause I'm a woman / Phenomenally. / Phenomenal woman, / That's me."

Reciting that extraordinary poem created a gentle opening for us, a way into a deeper conversation about what it means to be a woman, and that, at least for a moment, made the future a little less daunting.

The beauty in that room at Phoenix House stemmed from the collective witnessing of another person visibly overcoming a challenge. We are most lovable when we are vulnerable. But the feeling of shared victory was episodic. Everyone but me had to wake up the next morning and recommit to the grind of rehabilitation. The work of personal transformation can be brutal. Daily practices can supplement small victories at the edges if only to remind ourselves and each other that we are good, that we are not alone. Otherwise, the work can feel too hard.

And what of those who are committing to reforming entire systems, not only their own lives (which can be difficult enough)? Those people require mastering a sense of personal grounding, as well as the business practices needed to make a change process succeed. On both counts, there are few examples like Dr. Govindappa Venkataswamy, founder of India's venerable Aravind Eye Care System. At age thirty, he was crippled with rheumatoid arthritis, yet he did not allow the disease or anything else to hold him back. Instead, he dedicated himself first to overcoming his physical ailments and then to becoming one of the most highly skilled surgeons in India.

At fifty-eight, the age when his peers faced mandatory retirement, Dr. V left the Indian civil service and embarked on a quest to end treatable blindness. He had seen the toll of blindness on his fellow citizens, especially the poor, who could not afford cataract surgery. He also understood the nourishment that can come from serving others and knew he had a gift to offer the world. Unfazed by his age, infirmities, or lack of significant financial resources, he just started.

In 1976, in a tiny house fitted with merely eleven beds in the south Indian town of Madurai, Dr. V founded Aravind Eye Care System, resolving to provide eye care services to all people regardless of their ability to pay. Then he went in search of the most elegant and efficient solutions to bringing cataract surgery, affordably, to *millions* of India's poorest—and to do so with a financially sustaining business model.

I first met Dr. V in 2002. He had driven himself to meet me at Madurai's tiny airport and was standing at the gate leaning on a wooden walking cane, his hair thick and white, a mischievous twinkle in his eye. As he drove me into town, he described his beloved Aravind Eye Care System like a young man excited by ideas and possibilities and recounted how he acquired knowledge wherever he could find it.

"We had to build a system that was fast, low-cost, high-quality, and accessible to the poor," Dr. V explained.

He told us how in his search for effective business models, he was taken by the American fast-food company McDonald's, which broke down operational processes into distinct, repeatable practices. The Aravind Eye Hospital would do the same, he decided. Surgeons stand in the operating theater and do what they do best: perform cataract surgeries. Trained health workers prepare patients, deliver them to the operating theater, and then take them to the recovery rooms, where other health workers support the post-op processes.

Had Dr. Venkataswamy integrated only McDonald's values of efficiency and accountability, his business model could have made him a very wealthy man. But Aravind's mission was to eradicate blindness among the poor, and Dr. Venkataswamy believed in the interconnection of all things. His spiritual philosophy undergirded a business model that was driven, first and foremost, to provide eye care to all people, regardless of their ability to pay, and to treat the poorest with the respect and dignity they deserved.

In other words, Dr. V's spiritual philosophy, which put the poor first, required toughness and discipline that far exceeded the skills and resolve of businesses pursuing profits alone. That same philosophy sustained his focus on his mission for forty years. In turn, Dr. Venkataswamy integrated those values into every operational aspect of this nonconforming eye hospital system.

Aravind Eye Hospitals remains one of the most powerful pro-poor business models I have ever encountered. "It is not enough to provide essential eye care to the blind for free," Thulsi Ravilla, the genius businessman who worked closely with Dr. V, explained to me. "Our starting point was ensuring that *all* people could access eye care. If you want to serve the poorest, you have to consider and integrate their costs of giving up a day's earnings and paying bus fare to and from the hospital." The result of Aravind's efforts has been to deliver world-class health care to more than fifty-five million low-income patients, half of whom do not pay.

Dr. Venkataswamy's spiritual grounding kept him focused on creating an operational model that would succeed only if it effectively served the poor. Taking time daily to replenish and renew his commitment to his mission, he was up well before the sun each day; spent hours in reflection and meditation, reciting Sri Aurobindo's epic poem *Savitri*; and reminded himself that divinity exists in the interconnection of all things.

To meet Dr. V was to experience a man who remained present in the here and now, focused on human potential with no trace of despondency. It was impossible to refrain from smiling around him, as his spirit and unbridled laughter lit up a room. In his own words, "Intelligence and capability are not enough. There must be the joy of doing something beautiful." For more than thirty years, Dr. V sustained his vision with the wisdom of an elder and the curiosity of a child. Though he died in 2006, his legacy is alive in the minds and vision of millions who have been changed for the better because he existed.

Dr. Venkataswamy confidently wove his understanding of the material world and its realities with his unabashed belief in human interconnectedness and dignity. Whether you are fighting to solve poverty, to heal the earth, to reform the criminal justice system, or pursuing a host of other aims, there will inevitably be moments when the more established world makes you feel like a fool for "not understanding business" or "being soft" or for trying too hard. Remember, again, in those times that real love is a hard skill. I also hope you can find rituals, whether religious or decidedly nonreligious, to sustain and connect you more fully to the realization that we are on this fragile planet for a short time, that we are here together, that all we have is one another. And that you are enough.

I've been moved to see young people breathe new life into ancient rituals. Fahad Afridi, a Pashtun Acumen fellow in Pakistan, told me that when he touches his head to the ground in prayer, he is reminded to pause and feel gratitude for the earth, for all we are given. In this I heard echoes of an Acumen India teammate, Karuna Jain, who shared her family's tradition of starting each day by feeding seeds to birds outside their home as a touchstone for our interdependence. Others pursue yoga or meditation; they might read or listen music, or dance, or walk or run in nature. What matters is pausing long enough to pay attention, to hear yourself, to bring a small respite to the day.

There are a thousand ways to reconnect to the here and now. The Jesuits practice a daily examen, a quick check-in with themselves, once at noon and again at the end of the day. I have adapted a shortened four-step version. In the morning, set your intention for what you hope to do or how you hope to be during the day. At noon and/or in the evening, step back and assess how you are doing and what you're learning from both success and failure. Third, forgive yourself for where you failed. And fourth, express gratitude. When I remember to incorporate this short practice into my day, I feel calmer, more focused, more grounded.

There is wisdom in practices that entreat us to pause, to breathe, to contemplate what we are here to do. It takes only a moment to remind myself that my very life depends on the millions who toil planting the food we eat, making the clothes we wear—and that our interconnection demands some sort of reciprocity. I try to start most days reading a poem—Rumi, Hafiz, Mary Oliver, Rainer Maria Rilke, Seamus Heaney, Maya Angelou, and Marie Howe are among my favorites. Poets trade in the universal, the transcendent, the awe-inspiring simplicity of the world. The silence between their words is almost a meditation itself.

My most consistent and timeworn ritual is to go for a morning run. I love to feel my body come alive as the world wakes up, to breathe in the colors of the sky, to mark the changes in seasons, to explore new places and rekindle delight in being alive. No matter how bad things get—and thirty-plus years of working on poverty is a long time—a run restores my spirit and readies me for the day. Of course, these are simply *my* practices employed to help sustain my life's work and hopefully make me a better leader. Whoever you are and whatever you do, I hope you can find your own ways to make time to nourish your spirit and find a sense of wholeness even when the world is trying to break you. I hope you balance action with time for reflection.

A decade ago, when I published *The Blue Sweater*, I was surprised to receive so many letters from readers who voiced their desire to be of use. None moved me, though, like the long text message I received from a man named Kevin George Otieno, a resident of the Kibera slum in Nairobi. Kevin had found the book through an Acumen fellow, Suraj Sudhakar, who was working at a company that operated pay-per-use city toilets according to a different model from that of Sanergy. Kevin was hanging around the toilet operation, asking about Suraj's work. Eventually, Suraj offered him a copy of my book—on the condition that Kevin write and send me a review.

A few weeks later, I received a long text from Kevin: "I'm just like you," he wrote. "Like you, I have failed many times. I was only able to complete third grade. I am HIV-positive and out of work. But if you have failed in your life and still made so many changes, then it gives me hope that I can, too. And just like you, I also want to help bridge the gap between rich and poor."

I was speechless, glad that documenting my own failures could help someone so different from me overcome some of his fears. After reflecting for a day or so, I wrote Kevin back. "If you'd like to give my book to other friends who might enjoy reading it, I'm happy to send copies to you," I wrote. "But I'd like to hold a book club to hear from your friends."

"Deal," Kevin replied. "I'll take a hundred."

So began the Blue Sweater Book Club, organized by Kevin, his friend Alex Sanguti, and five others. Despite their hardscrabble lives (selling eggs on the street, working as laborers, sometimes earning the equivalent of about thirty cents for a day's work), they each found time to distribute the one hundred books to fellow slum residents.

Driving through Kibera's muddy alleyways the day of the book club meeting, I was unprepared for what I saw. More than a hundred people were crammed into Mama Hamza's community center, a corrugated-tin box of a room outfitted with white plastic chairs. I felt overcome with shyness, acutely aware of my privilege while writing about poor people living in slums like this one. I desperately did not want to let this group down.

The self-proclaimed "controller," Kevin kicked off the event, cheekily warning the other club members that he would cut off anyone who was long-winded. "This is about the future," he proclaimed.

Alex went next, speaking about experiences that had taught him that tribalism and nepotism were barriers to one's goals in life.

"If you ate a meal or slept with a roof over your head last night," he said, "remember that many have it much worse than you do."

The two were a hard act to follow. The slum dwellers asked many questions—how to start a business, how to find funding for a local project—and I did my best to respond. Then a young woman, slender, short, and muscular, wearing jeans and a dark cotton blouse, piped up from the back:

"I'm a teenager and a single mother. I have no money, and I'm HIV-positive. How can I be a leader? Who will follow me?"

I stammered through a nonresponse, citing Jesus and Muhammad, and then some people whose names no one there recognized. I was embarrassed to have drawn a blank, as I knew so many audacious, competent leaders of humble backgrounds from this young woman's city. But at just that moment, out of the crowd, a beautiful woman in a flaming red dress stepped forward. I recognized her at once: Jane. We'd met through Jamii Bora, the Nairobi-based microfinance organization. Her story was full of backbreaking challenges, yet she was a survivor.

Jane spoke directly to the skeptical young woman, from her own experiences. "If you had known me ten years ago, you would not believe I am here today," she said. "I was a prostitute for seven years before I came to Jamii Bora. By then, I was also a single mother with HIV. Jamii Bora taught me to sew, and now I am a tailor. My children are happy. And I feel so lucky that I volunteer at the health clinic to counsel people who have just discovered they are HIV-positive.

"I grew up very poor. I could not follow my dreams to be a doctor because of what life gave me. But now, in some ways, I'm better. You see, doctors, they give out pills. But me, I give out hope."

Jane began to turn around and then stopped, looking again at the agitated teen mom. "Everyone can be a leader," she said. "Don't make excuses."

The larger conversation continued, and I tried to direct more of the queries toward the other people standing in the room, but the questions to me continued. And just like Kevin in his original text to me, many people started their queries with the phrase "I'm just like you, but . . ."

I started to feel like a fraud.

"I appreciate your generosity and your humility," I finally said, "but the truth is, you are not just like me. I live in a good neighborhood in New York City and attended some of the country's best schools. I hold an American passport and my skin is white. I travel around the world and know the freedom in my privilege. I hope I never take it for granted, but my life is very different."

Mama Hamza, the irrepressible entrepreneur in charge of the community center, broke into a huge grin. "We know that," she said. "Yes, you are privileged. But still, you fight for issues we fight. You care about the changes we want to make. You fail and sometimes succeed—like we do. You see yourself as part of us. This is what makes us like you—and you like us."

On the way back to my hotel, I shared a van with Catherine Casey Nanda and Jocelyn Wyatt, two younger colleagues who have since become close friends. We drove in silence through Kibera's still-muddy streets, each of us lost in thought, my heart lodged in my throat. Something had happened in Mama Hamza's center. We had all shown up simply as ourselves, to learn and gather in communion.

I was no longer that young woman trying and failing to lead a diverse group of young Americans when I could not fully acknowledge my own identity. I wondered what had taken me so long to remove every mask I'd ever worn and finally show up as no one else but my truest self.

The transcendence of that experience at Mama Hamza's was another reminder that we are part of something bigger than ourselves. Instead of kneeling in a grandly lit cathedral or a mosque with soaring ceilings, we stood together in a dark, makeshift community center in an impoverished slum, yet the ground in Kibera on that night felt no less sacred. That precious moment continues to feed my commitment all these years later. That evening, I was able to acknowledge the beauty inside myself and, in so doing, make it easier for others to acknowledge what was good and beautiful inside them. The theologian Howard Thurman has called that quiet recognition "the sound of the genuine." When we reveal our most genuine selves, not only do we invite the same from others, but the choice to work toward something beyond ourselves becomes inevitable.

Finally, when times are terrible—and few of us escape living without experiencing tragedies and sorrows—there is sustenance in beauty manifested in service, in the arts, in rebuilding what has been destroyed. In 1994, I had the immense privilege of sitting alone with fabled dancers of Cambodia's Royal Ballet at their modest studio in Phnom Penh. During the mid- to late 1970s, under the Pol Pot regime, the Khmer Rouge army murdered over a million Cambodians, targeting intellectuals and artists. Just thirty classical dancers survived the war, and only three remained living when I visited to learn about their work as part of the Philanthropy Workshop, a program I had created at the Rockefeller Foundation.

A petite gray-haired woman dressed in wide-legged yellow trousers and a deep red jacket imparted her recollections of the refugee camps after the war. She was elegant and graceful, with a perfect carriage. "I would lie in my cot," she said softly, "and try to piece together the dances but could only hold on to fragments," she recalled. "You see, our dances have been passed down through each generation orally, for more than a thousand years. Only we, the dancers, held the keys to reviving this part of our nation's heritage. I desperately hoped that other dancers might still be alive, trying to remember, as I was." These women's recollections were links to the dances' revival—and their immortality.

Once the surviving dancers had found one another, they pledged to train their grandchildren's generation—their daughters' generation had already grown too old—in the ancient techniques of the Royal Ballet. She spoke calmly, slowly, her gaze straight at me while tears trickled down her face, not once lifting her hand to dry her cheeks.

Suddenly, little girls pranced into the studio for practice. Watching the class, I was mesmerized as the elderly women stood at the center of the room clapping to beguiling rhythms of age-old music played by old men with slender, creative hands sitting at the edge of the dance floor. Little fairy pixies pirouetted around the women, a circular rainbow of fluttering iridescent silks surrounding slender, wise old trees. The bland room metamorphosed into an enchanted garden.

After unimaginable bloodshed and loss, I thought to myself, there is dance. There is a new generation to teach. And in that new generation is a chance for rebirth. The elderly dancers, nearly annihilated, were honoring what was most beautiful about the nation's past and building it into the future, forging a hard-edged hope out of suffering, beauty, and faith.

Faith does not have to be religious, and prayer can take a thousand forms. We are on dangerous ground when "faith" becomes associated with political parties, or when nonbelievers are seen as heretics rather than seekers. A moral framework for an interdependent world has no place for religious practices that divide. What matters instead is that we agree to at least some shared moral principles that enable our collective human flourishing. In whatever form faith takes for you, I wish you a reservoir from which you can draw sustenance. May you find ways and rituals to remind you to be present in the world, to be grateful.

When you are broken or exhausted—and you will be—remember beauty, gratitude, faith, and love. Remember that in the struggle, there is a beauty that endures. Remember that there will be beauty in moments of tragedy as well as in times of shared celebration. But most important, remember that beauty is inside you, if you let it be.

Chapter 14

MANIFESTO

A few times a year, I run or walk uptown along New York City's Hudson River to pay homage to a hero from my childhood whose example has accompanied me throughout my life. At the entry to Riverside Park, under soaring oak trees, stands a giant-size bronze statue of Eleanor Roosevelt, human rights activist and one of America's most venerable First Ladies. Mrs. Roosevelt's figure, attired in a simple dress and a spring coat, leans casually against a boulder, her hand at her chin, her distinctive face in restive contemplation. Silently, I thank her for her service to her country and the world.

Because she dared, the world is a different place. Because she had the courage to stand for those who were excluded, my life as a woman is radically better than it would have been had I been born in her era. Because she maintained her faith in the goodness of people while having a front seat to one of the darkest times in human history, I try to assume that same goodness in others.

Mrs. Roosevelt embodied principles of moral leadership, renewing her commitment time and again to remake an imperfect world. If she harbored inner doubts, she nonetheless displayed a willingness to confront her fears and undertake exceedingly demanding and sometimes delicate tasks in service of her commitment to others. I can only imagine the tensions Mrs. Roosevelt had to balance—first, as a wife and First Lady who sometimes openly disagreed with her husband's policies; and second, as a leader who believed in and fought for the rights of African Americans, low-wage workers, and women in her country while also embracing the duties of America's responsibility to fight a world war. Hers was a public life with its own share of private pain, in which she grew in wisdom and effectiveness until the end of her days—because she tried.

* * *

As a young woman, Mrs. Roosevelt was not particularly aware of race issues in America. But as the wife of a president fighting a war over human rights in Europe, and with the encouragement of resolute African Americans willing to speak their own truths to power, she expanded her understanding. She listened. She took valiant, unpopular stands to push for expanded rights for African Americans. In return, she was called a Communist, a traitor, and, I'm sure, much worse. But as she practiced acts of moral courage, she became more courageous. And through it all, she lost neither her humility nor her audacity.

In 1946, the world was only beginning to recover from a war of murderous destruction: thirty million lives lost, many because they were deemed by some to be less valuable than others. A manifesto was called for to renew the world's most urgently needed values. Mrs. Roosevelt's crowning achievement was chairing the United Nations Commission on Human Rights. She played an influential role in drafting the

Universal Declaration of Human Rights, which in December 1948 the UN General Assembly proclaimed as the international standard for human rights. In it, Mrs. Roosevelt and her coauthors set forth a rights-based framework with the hope of protecting future generations from the horrors the world had just endured.

That Declaration, one of history's most aspirational expressions of what we owe one another as human beings, established human rights as a moral principle to be nourished and protected. The Declaration is based firmly on the equality of all human beings. By virtue of being born human, the document argues, every person should be guaranteed the right to be treated as nothing *less* than human. Consider the opening lines of its preamble: "Whereas recognition of the inherent dignity and of the equal and inalienable rights of all members of the human family is the foundation of freedom, justice and peace in the world." In this single principle, the immutable value of human dignity stands front and center.

Without doubt, seventy years later, most countries still fall short of meeting some of the most basic rights, whether it be the right to equal protection of the law or the right to education and a "fair and adequate living standard." Read the Declaration's principles and it becomes impossible to resist shaking your head at how far the world remains from the aspirations inscribed in it many decades ago. Reread it and you might discover gaps where more aspiration is in order.

Some disagree with the Declaration's core premise. Cynics and strongmen may scoff that the Declaration of Human Rights is hopelessly idealistic or unrealistic. Others would willingly trade off political freedoms (of free speech or the protection of minorities, for instance) to know their economic rights are protected above all. In unstable times, humans' fear of scarcity, hurt, and loss causes too many of us to lean on the false security of privilege by excluding or blaming others.

While imperfect, the Declaration has endured as one of the most important documents of all time. It has been translated into more than 330 languages, and while not legally enforceable, it has assumed a moral and political significance, inspiring generations to protect the oppressed and those who speak out on their behalf. It has served as the basis for constitutions and treaties, setting forth standards for expanding what is owed every human being if we hope to live with true dignity.

I am far from being an expert on Eleanor Roosevelt, yet I wonder what she would have thought of the early decades of the twenty-first century. I imagine she'd have been pleased by the continued expansion of individual rights and freedoms, and astonished by how individualistic yet interdependent we have become. I'd guess she'd have been curious about the juxtaposition of the possibilities and perils of a technologically connected world. She would almost certainly have recognized the continued relevance of her belief that human rights begin "in small places, close to home—so close and so small that they cannot be seen on any maps of the world. Yet they are the world of the individual person; the neighborhood he lives in; the school or college he attends; the factory, farm, or office where he works."

Though our greatest threats are divergent from those Eleanor Roosevelt's generation faced, in many countries around the world there is a chilling symmetry in the spreading fear of the "other." The burgeoning refugee crisis prompts one to ask: who is responsible for masses of people who, no longer able to survive on their lands, have no choice but to leave behind everything and everyone dear to them? Climate change, the phenomenon most critical to humanity's shared future, was not even contemplated in the mid-twentieth century. The earth is witnessing the extermination of species at a shocking rate, imperiling our food supplies, our oceans, and the equilibrium and beauty of nature. A new declaration infused with the moral imagination of a new generation might consider not only our rights, then, but our *responsibilities*, recognizing that if we do not sustain the earth, human rights will die along with our species.

In a time of low trust, such a manifesto will not come from on high—certainly not one that will guide our daily actions. Yet we face threats that carry within them perilous consequences and untold opportunities—not for some, but for the human race as a whole—challenges requiring each of us to renew the values of human dignity, basic rights, and decency. When we finally muster the courage to change ourselves, only then can we change the world.

Freedom does not exist without constraint. Saying aloud those values that bind us, whether we start with our families, our organizations, our communities, or our nations, is a start. Aspiring to live those values is the next step. Within each of us lies the basis for the only revolution that will save us: a moral revolution.

In 2011, we at Acumen put into writing our deepest beliefs about the work we do to use investment as a tool for social change and to build a community of remarkable people— social entrepreneurs, fellows, philanthropists, impact investors, committed students, and agents of change. I offer you Acumen's manifesto here simply as one example of a declaration of principles that guide a community dedicated to being part of the moral revolution called for by our divided world. This declaration of principles is aspirational, but it has become a moral compass, a daily reminder of who we *aim* to be and who we *practice* being:

It starts by standing with the poor. Listening to voices unheard, and recognizing potential where others see despair.

It demands investing as a means, not an end, daring to go where markets have failed and aid has fallen short. It makes capital work for us, not control us.

It thrives on moral imagination: the humility to see the world as it is, and the audacity to imagine the world as it could be. It's having the ambition to learn at the edge, the wisdom to admit failure, and the courage to start again.

It requires patience and kindness, resilience and grit: a hard-edged hope. It's leadership that rejects complacency, breaks through bureaucracy, and challenges corruption. Doing what's right, not what's easy.

It's the radical idea of creating hope in a cynical world. Changing the way the world tackles poverty and building a world based on dignity.

Acumen's manifesto has served our global community well. The phrase "It starts by standing with the poor" confronts us in every investment meeting and at every management session as we grapple with how to ensure that our work favorably impacts low-income populations. The idea of "investing as a means, not an end" requires that we balance financial returns with the goals we seek. Balancing patience with urgency, calling out our own failures, committing to resilience, yet knowing when to call it quits—our commitment to these values sets standards that better us.

And we're far from perfect: though a sense of humor, of joy, and a willingness to forgive ourselves and others are not included in the manifesto, they nourish and sustain us.

My team and board have had many discussions about the word *poor*, and how language can be limiting. Ultimately, Acumen has maintained the word *poor* because we see poverty simply as a lack of choice and opportunity; the word says nothing about a person's character. Indeed, some of the richest lives I have ever encountered have been lives of scarce means, while others with the financial advantages of kings have been desperately lacking in spirit.

Although we don't mention the earth in our manifesto, Acumen's community assumes that if you care about poverty, you will also focus on climate change, which continues to harm the vulnerable disproportionately more than the wealthy. This set of guiding principles has provided steady grounding, especially in those times when solid land is unavailable.

I have also observed with awe how embodying values can ripple across lands and oceans to unexpected places. Don't underestimate the impact you can have as a parent, a teacher, a colleague, an organization builder. When I started Acumen, I dreamed of touching the lives of millions, though the actual *community* we directly worked with was relatively small.

If you include only the philanthropists, entrepreneurs, and fellows with whom Acumen interacts directly, then two decades after its founding our work reaches thousands. If you include the participants who have taken our online courses for social change, Acumen's principles have affected hundreds of thousands. But if you count the low-income people whose lives are tangibly different because a community of individuals decided they could do more for the world together than any one of them could accomplish alone, our efforts have impacted hundreds of millions.

To be of use, a manifesto based in a moral framework fit for the twenty-first century must connect with values that transcend nation, culture, religion, race, and class. Identifying a minimum set of values, though essential, is not always straightforward. Sometimes, in quiet moments, I've reflected on how many people in Acumen's community were raised to hate other members within our global circle. Whether with fellows, entrepreneurs, or the customers our companies serve, I'm regularly in conversation with people whose parents taught them that certain neighbors were "bad" or "evil." The global community comprises groups of deeply wounded people from places or of ethnicities, genders, or sexual identities under grave threat of persecution.

Yet cutting across every line that attempts to divide us is the growing recognition that we are bound to one another by virtue of our shared humanity and quest for dignity. I've been inspired by many people who grew up in communities that rejected other traditions but are now choosing to embrace a universal truth: there is divinity in each of us, and we are connected to something greater than ourselves.

And whether you believe that dignity comes from God or is inherent simply in our having been born human, the end result is the same. Every one of us deserves to be seen, to be respected, to determine his or her own life. Every one of us is owed a fighting chance to flourish.

From the beginning, my partners and I built Acumen as a deliberately diverse community, not for its own sake but so that we could use that diversity to know and to learn from one another how to navigate the growing tensions in our world.

We wanted to affirm our differences without erasing them, arriving at a sense of wholeness based on commonly shared values.

That commitment to one another and to shared values requires a willingness to confront obstacles to listening, to seeing, to making true human connection. The work of building our community requires being open to other faiths, cultures, and traditions, to celebrating what is most essential in each of them while building the courage to speak up about that which no longer serves. We commit ourselves to being members of a single human family, beyond any nation or religion, caste or tribe. This work is difficult and it is long, but it is the work of the moral revolution, the only way to build a future that will sustain us.

Your organization or business might work from different foundational principles than Acumen. The point is to reflect and put your purpose and values into words to serve as your own compass for decisions and actions, not only as an organization but as individuals.

Statements of values can guide actions and reinforce bonds of community—if they are *lived*. I've seen religious communities mask terrible acts with beautiful words from sacred texts, and I've witnessed philanthropists make change in one area of their lives while engaging in unethical practices elsewhere. To unite any group, let alone the world, in common purpose requires role models and business models that demonstrate values made manifest.

Muhammad Ali, an Acumen Pakistan fellow, is one such role model who relentlessly lives his values. I first met him in 2014, while leading a two-day seminar with his cohort of twenty fellows. This group of fellows and I again used literature as a springboard to conversation aimed at clarifying each individual's values, as well as identifying common beliefs held by this very diverse group of human beings.

When we first introduced ourselves, I was struck by Muhammad Ali's unassuming manner. He wore simple wire-frame glasses, his dark hair combed to the side, his mustache neatly trimmed, his button-down shirt and khaki trousers perfectly pressed. He spoke broken English in a soft voice that made him appear a bit shy at first. I imagined him working in an accountant's office. This could not have been further from the truth.

Once he opened his mouth, Muhammad Ali quickly impressed me with the quality of his ideas, grounded in ancient texts, and his commitment to putting his ideals into action. His values were based unyieldingly in the inherent worth of every child and an insistence that it was society's duty to protect all children.

By the time I met him, Muhammad Ali had spent twenty years rescuing children caught in the dark world of human trafficking. In 2004, he'd founded Roshni Helpline, to identify and rescue the missing children of the dispossessed. Muhammad Ali spoke with understandable anger about sexual assault, false adoption, prostitution, child labor—just a few of the myriad reasons a child goes missing in Karachi every day.

Muhammad Ali railed against the inequitable system that rallied the police, media, and community members to search for a single missing child of privilege while thousands of poor children who disappeared each year across the country drew little to no notice; they were left to experience their terror alone. Few resources, either philanthropic or governmental, focused on the children who lived at society's furthest edges.

Fighting human trafficking requires confronting the ugliest parts of ourselves, sides that many would rather not see.

To better understand how Muhammad Ali's values translated into results, in 2017 I drove with Acumen's Pakistan director, Ayesha Khan, to a Karachi slum area known for high levels of insecurity and violence and climbed a pale-blue staircase to the small second-story office of Roshni Helpline.

There, Muhammad Ali recounted how his mission to protect vulnerable children had led him to discover one of his most deeply held values: the power of a diverse community. "In the beginning, our organization had little money or staff," he explained, "and I soon recognized that if we were going to find a lost child, we could only do it with the full support of the community we were trying to serve." He ultimately called upon the police and relied on a complex informant system of thousands of local volunteers, including shopkeepers, street children, and Karachi's transgender community.

Transgender community members, a highly visible but discriminated group, have been fundamental to Roshni's success. Though they can be seen begging on streets and dancing at weddings in Karachi, transgender folks typically exist at the margins, with little access to jobs or income, living in informal housing with "chosen families" of people like them. Where others regarded transgender people as outsiders, Muhammad Ali recognized them as potential partners. "Traffickers often move children through underground routes that include bus stations, where transgender people can often be found. They were willing to help and have been our best volunteers."

During our visit, I had the privilege of sitting with several of Roshni's transgender volunteers. The group leader, Hina Pathani, wore a flowered *shalwar kameez*, her dark hair pulled back into a bun, tendrils framing her face. She explained that while she and other transgender volunteers had little money, they took great pride in their work. "I love my country," Hina said. "I want to be known for contributing, for doing something that makes me proud, and not to be seen as less than others."

Muhammad Ali set free the potential of community members who collectively became the superpower enabling Roshni's success. To date, the organization has saved nearly four thousand people, most of whom are children. Only through enlisting the help of the marginal and vulnerable could Muhammad Ali succeed, finding the strength to do what traditional child protection systems could not.

Muhammad Ali knows that four thousand people may not sound like a lot to outsiders, but each of those children represents a family. Each of those children represents a life to be lived. Muhammad Ali's work, which reveals the best of human conscientiousness countering the worst of human depravity, reminds me of lines from the poem "The Pedagogy of Conflict," by the human rights activist and Irish theologian Pádraig Ó Tuama:

> When I was a child,
> I learnt to count to five:
> One, two, three, four, five.
> But these days, I've been counting lives, so I count
> One life.
> One life.
> One life.
> One life.
> One life.

In a world that too often views our most indigent children as throwaways, Muhammad Ali is a candle burning to ensure that we behold the unseen.

Despite his local effectiveness, Muhammad Ali lacked access to financial and human resources to expand his reach. This is where our responsibility for extending social capital to voices unheard cannot be overestimated. Since becoming associated with Acumen, Roshni Helpline has worked with no fewer than ten fellows who've volunteered services in marketing, communications, technology, and government affairs. A few months after I visited, the Acumen team took a small delegation of our philanthropic partners from Pakistan and the United States to see Muhammad Ali's work firsthand. A few of the locals had never been to the part of town where Roshni worked; nor had they ever had a real conversation with transgender folks.

By the end of the day's visit, the philanthropists had agreed to fund Roshni's entire budget for the following three years. Wealthy individuals signed on as ambassadors, spreading the word about Roshni's work and raising enough money to build a safe house for traumatized children. Putting the Acumen manifesto's values into action, the philanthropists encouraged Muhammad Ali to be audacious in his plans, yet they maintained the humility to listen to what the founder of Roshni most needed rather than imposing their own desires.

Momentum built. The Karachi police requested that Roshni Helpline train its officers to be of better support. A local paint company sponsored artists to paint portraits of the missing children on the elaborately decorated trucks that drive across the country—and within months, a child who'd been missing for seven years was rescued. Fifteen years after Muhammad Ali founded Roshni Helpline, Pakistan's Supreme Court is making the kidnapping of children under age eighteen a cognizable crime, which means the police now will have the authority to investigate.

By valuing not only the individual but the communities that support that person, Muhammad Ali has tapped into many people's urge to be of use. The transgender volunteers along with philanthropists, designers, marketers, artists, a public relations company, and others are demonstrating what is possible when a diverse group of individuals unites to reweave the torn fabric of society. When we do this, we recognize not only our powers to heal, but our entanglement with one another. We gain the chance to remind ourselves that we are in this world together, that all we have is each other, that, to use words of the poet Gwendolyn Brooks, "We are each other's harvest."

James Kassaga Arainaitwe is an Acumen fellow from Western Uganda who lost both parents and all four of his siblings to disease, including AIDS, before he was ten years old. Kassaga (his preferred name) was raised by his grandmother, a gentle battle-ax of a woman fiercely focused on giving her grandchild two treasures no one could take from him: self-discipline and an education. When local schooling options ran out at age eleven, she put Kassaga on a bus alone for the three-hundred-kilometer journey to the childhood village in southwestern Uganda where the nation's President Museveni maintained his personal home. Kassaga's grandmother figured the small boy would somehow find a champion to help him meet the president's family and secure a scholarship to school.

His grandmother's risk paid off. Because of his tenacity, Kassaga met the country's First Lady, and not only found a place to learn in Uganda, but went on to attend Florida State University on a full scholarship.

As an Acumen fellow, Kassaga worked in Bangalore, India, at Gayathri Vasudevan's LabourNet, the company described in chapter 3 that provides effective vocational and entrepreneurial training for low-income workers. On weekends, Kassaga would volunteer at a school for low-income students. That experience reconnected him with what had initially saved him: education.

Dots connected: During his time in India, Kassaga met Acumen fellows who'd worked with Teach for India, a part of the powerful Teach for All network founded by Wendy Kopp. They began a brainstorm that would expand to include other fellows who were designers and strategists. Soon, Kassaga, aided by an Indian community of trusted partners, conceptualized and created Teach for Uganda.

In times of growing fears and divides, citizens are the future of a new global diplomacy. Values-driven communities can expedite making global ambassadors of all of us. The India fellows had forged a bond with Kassaga over their shared experiences with Acumen and their belief that every child deserves a basic quality education. As Kassaga later wrote me, "Their tireless sacrifice for an organization in a country they've never stepped foot in reveals more than just their love for me. It shows the interconnectedness of humanity. To them, I was not seen as the 'other.' I became their brother, and they became my sisters and brothers. It is the African spiritual ideal of *ubuntu*, or 'human kindness,' that forever unites me with them."

Kassaga is supported in myriad ways by Acumen's Ugandan fellows, who provide him with training, connections, a needed ear, and what we at Acumen affectionately call a "one-armed hug"—enough support to stand with someone, but not so much that you disable them. With the support of a local and global community behind him, Kassaga is primed to make Teach for Uganda a success, unleashing the energies of a new generation and bringing back the best of what other regions have to offer to the country he calls home.

A revolution of values is one that necessarily relies on

countless, immeasurable daily heroic acts. Unified in the pursuit of dignity, we can serve in a thousand ways. Fortified by
one another, we can choose to celebrate role models who help
others succeed. Strengthened by a commitment to shared values, we can build meaningful, productive relationships across
lines of difference.

Consider writing your own manifesto. It should start with
what is most important to you, the world you want to create—in
your school, local community, or company. Next, consider the
means you will need to achieve those ends. What are the obstacles you face? The tensions you must hold? What kind of person
do you want to be as you live your purpose? If you can envision
your horizon, you can build a pathway there. It will inevitably be
a long, twisting one, sometimes turning back on itself entirely.
But I hope your path will be joined by many others, drawn to
that mission, purpose, and values to which you subscribe.

All of us are needed for a moral revolution. It doesn't matter where you live, the size of your bank account, or what
you do for a living. The world needs you to flex, to stretch to
uncomfortable levels, to build your moral imagination, to listen more deeply, to reckon with your sense of identity, and to
open yourself up to understanding the layered inconsistencies
and differing perspectives of others. It requires each of us to
partner better, to tell stories that matter, and to embrace the
beautiful struggle.

Critically, a revolution of morals requires each of us to
rethink success, asking ourselves whether we are doing enough
to serve others, whether we are enabling others to help themselves, whether we are kind. We must find the courage to recognize, integrate, and accept the light and dark sides of ourselves
so that we can bolster and integrate our larger communities.
Finally, we must have faith that we can solve our biggest

problems, trusting that we can bridge our divides *because* we are connected, because we can see one another, because our shared destiny is dependent on the dignity of every one of us.

Whoever you are and whatever you do, the world needs you to lead. There will be times when happiness may feel elusive and the horizon impossible to reach. But remember that each day, we wake up to another chance to renew the world. Daily, we have a choice to recommit to the work we came to do. Daily, we can reconstitute the promise of hard-edged hope.

After the horrendous terrorist attacks in the fall of 2015 in Paris and California, Baheira Khusheim, an Acumen fellow from Saudi Arabia, wrote me an email from a hospital in Houston, Texas, where she was accompanying her father as he underwent treatment for cancer. The Saudi consulate had called her, she wrote, to ask her to be cautious when moving about. Friends suggested she remove her headscarf so as to avoid facing discrimination. Muslims, they said, were at risk of counterattacks.

After some consideration, Baheira decided, "If I do not stand up to show the world a different face of my religion, who will?" The irony of sitting in a cancer ward where so many women covered their heads with scarves was not lost on Baheira. She could wear a scarf in solidarity with the cancer patients, she reasoned. Why couldn't she wear one out of respect for her religion?

The following day, Baheira, her head covered, made a trip to a nearby grocery store. The young Saudi woman self-consciously was walking down the vegetable aisle when a stranger rushed up to her. His intense expression sent her into a mild panic. Then Baheira noticed the bouquet of flowers in the stranger's hand. "I bought them to bring to my house," he explained. "But when I saw you here in my hometown, I thought I'd give these flowers to you instead. Thank you for your courage in showing your Muslim identity during this difficult time."

About a year later, I was invited to Saudi Arabia to launch the Arabic translation of my first book, a gift made possible by our four Saudi fellows and scores of young people who felt close to Acumen's mission. Many people, including some from Acumen's own community, expressed disapproval that I would travel to the country given its poor human rights record. But I was there to engage with young people who hungered to be part of the world.

Three of the Acumen fellows there, Yousuf Alguwaifli, Shahd Al Shehail, and Lujain Al Ubaid, hosted me in Riyadh, introducing me to many young people who impressed me with their knowledge of other cultures. Many expressed a deep desire to help change their country while also keeping and sharing the traditions that made them proud, such as a shared commitment to family and the region's unmatched hospitality to guests.

On my final morning in Riyadh, I took a taxi to the airport. Though I'd previously been welcomed graciously by everyone I'd encountered, the driver treated me disdainfully, almost shouting at me to adjust my *hijab* and *abaya*, the black head-scarf and gown worn there to cover a woman's head and body. Sitting silently, I felt humiliated, reminded for a brief moment what the powerless experience a hundred times a day. Then, as I was putting my bags through security, a surly worker harassed me. I focused again on holding my composure, reminding myself not to allow his disrespect to inform my actions.

Nonetheless, I was shaken up by both incidents. I spotted a coffee shop in the terminal and made a beeline for the comfort of a latte. As I was standing in that line, a Saudi man approached me. He was carrying several boxes of fresh dates in his arms. I wondered what was coming next.

"Excuse me," he said, "but I watched that man attempt to humiliate you in the security line. You kept your grace through it, and I want to thank you for that. But watching the interaction made me feel ashamed. I don't want you to leave my country thinking you are not welcome. I don't want you to think that kind of behavior is acceptable to us."

I smiled and said thank you.

"Please," he continued, "take these dates home. They are full of sweetness. Take them as a gift from myself and my fellow Saudis. Enjoy them with your friends and family."

I thanked him profusely but tried to refuse. Laughing, I added, "Plus, there must be twenty pounds of dates in your arms. I can't even carry all those!"

He insisted I take them, helping devise a way for me to hold them more easily. And then he added, "Knowing you have them will do me good. Don't you think we need reminders of how much love is out there?"

Yes, I said. I do. I do.

As Eleanor Roosevelt wrote long ago, the work of renewing a world based on extending dignity to every being on the planet begins in small places, close to home. As we go through life on this tiny, blue planet, the only home we know, imagine the changes that might arise if we each took a step toward making it a home in which all of us could participate, where each person could flourish with peace and justice and a sense of wholeness for many, many generations to come.

The world is waiting for you.

SELECTED READINGS

Angelou, Maya. "Phenomenal Woman." In *Maya Angelou: The Complete Poetry*. New York: Random House, 2015.

Arendt, Hannah. *Eichmann in Jerusalem: A Report on the Banality of Evil*. New York: Penguin Classics, 2006.

Brooks, David. *The Road to Character*. New York: Random House, 2015.

Brooks, David. *The Second Mountain: The Quest for a Moral Life*. New York: Random House, 2019.

Brooks, Gwendolyn. "Paul Robeson." In *The Essential Gwendolyn Brooks*. New York: Library of America, 2005.

Collier, Paul. *The Future of Capitalism: Facing the New Anxieties*. New York: Harper, 2018.

Dalio, Ray. *Principles: Life and Work*. New York: Simon & Schuster, 2017.

Eliot, T. S. *Four Quartets*. Boston: Mariner, 1968.

Frankl, Viktor E. *Man's Search for Meaning*. Boston: Beacon, 2006.

Gardner, John W. *Self-Renewal: The Individual and the Innovative Society*. Brattleboro, VT: Echo Point, 2015.

Giridharadas, Anand. *Winners Take All: The Elite Charade of Changing the World*. New York: Knopf, 2018.

Godin, Seth. *The Dip: A Little Book That Teaches You When to Quit (and When to Stick)*. New York: Portfolio, 2007.

Godin, Seth. *Linchpin: Are You Indispensable?* New York: Portfolio, 2011.

Hafiz. *The Gift.* Translated by Daniel Ladinsky, New York: Penguin, 1999.

Haidt, Jonathan. *The Righteous Mind: Why Good People Are Divided by Politics and Religion.* New York: Pantheon, 2012.

Harari, Yuval Noah. *Sapiens: A Brief History of Humankind.* New York: Harper Perennial, 2018.

Havel, Václav. *The Power of the Powerless: Citizens against the State in Central Eastern Europe.* New York: Routledge, 1985.

Helminski, Kabir, ed. *The Rumi Collection: An Anthology of Translations of Mevlâna Jalâluddin Rumi.* Boston: Shambhala, 2005.

Howe, Marie. *Magdalene: Poems.* New York: W. W. Norton, 2017.

King, Martin Luther, Jr. "Letter from Birmingham Jail." In *I Have a Dream.* Logan, IA: Perfection Learning, 2007.

Lowney, Chris. *Heroic Leadership: Best Practices from a 450-Year-Old Company That Changed the World.* Chicago: Loyola Press, 2005.

Lukianoff, Greg and Jonathan Haidt. *The Coddling of the American Mind: How Good Intentions and Bad Ideas Are Setting Up a Generation for Failure.* New York: Penguin, 2018.

Maalouf, Amin. *In the Name of Identity: Violence and the Need to Belong.* Translated by Barbara Bray. New York: Arcade, 2001.

Machiavelli, Niccolò. *The Prince.* Edited and translated by David Wootton. Indianapolis, IN: Hackett Publishing, 1995.

Mandela, Nelson. "I Am Prepared to Die." Testimony, Rivonia Trial, April 20, 1964, Pretoria, South Africa. Nelson Mandela Foundation, http://db.nelsonmandela.org/speeches/pub_view.asp?pg=item&ItemID =NMS010&txtstr=prepared to die.

Oliver, Mary. "Mysteries, Yes." In *Evidence: Poems.* Boston: Beacon, 2009.

Ó Tuama, Pádraig. "The Pedagogy of Conflict." In *In the Shelter: Finding a Home in the World.* London: Hodder & Stoughton, 2015.

Ó Tuama, Pádraig. *Sorry for Your Troubles.* Norwich, UK: Canterbury Press, 2013.

Pagels, Elaine. *Why Religion?: A Personal Story.* New York: Ecco, 2018.

Plato, *The Republic.* Translated by Desmond Lee. New York: Penguin Classics, 2007.

Popova, Maria. *BrainPickings.org* blog.

Rohr, Richard. *Falling Upward: A Spirituality for the Two Halves of Life.* San Francisco: Jossey-Bass, 2011.

Rousseau, Jean-Jacques. *The Social Contract.* Translated by Maurice Cranston. New York: Penguin Classics, 1968.

Rumi, Jalal ad-Din. *The Essential Rumi.* New expanded edition. Translated by Coleman Barks. New York: HarperOne, 2004.

Sen, Amartya. *Development as Freedom.* New York: Anchor, 2000.

Smith, Adam. *The Theory of Moral Sentiments.* New York: Penguin Classics, 2009.

Solomon, Andrew. *Far from the Tree: Parents, Children, and the Search for Identity.* New York: Scribner, 2012.

Stevenson, Bryan. *Just Mercy: A Story of Justice and Redemption.* New York: Spiegel & Grau, 2014.

Tippett, Krista. *Becoming Wise: An Inquiry into the Mystery and Art of Living.* New York: Penguin, 2016.

Venkataraman, Bina. *The Optimist's Telescope: Thinking Ahead in a Reckless Age.* New York: Riverhead, 2019.

Whitman, Walt. *Song of Myself.* N.p.: Dover, 2001.

Yunus, Muhammad. *A World of Three Zeros: The New Economics of Zero Poverty, Zero Unemployment, and Zero Net Carbon Emissions.* New York: PublicAffairs, 2017.

ACKNOWLEDGMENTS

We make our lives with each other. This book has been nurtured by multitudes. To all of them I am grateful.

Thanks to my brilliant editor, Barbara Jones, and the great team at Holt. Barbara, you pushed me to uncomfortable places, edited with insight and care, and talked me off a few cliffs. And the book is better for it. Thanks, too, to Ruby Rose Lee and the copy editor, Jenna Dolan, who reviewed the manuscript. Thank you to my irrepressible agent Elyse Cheney and your team for believing in and fighting for this book. And for being dreamers who do.

Cyndi Stivers, you are a miracle. Thank you for accompanying me from the very first days of Sunflowers to the final editing with thrilling speed and surety. William Charnock, the shepherd, you always said yes, made my challenges yours, remained impossibly positive, and kept me sane. Bavidra Mohan, your thoughtful feedback illuminated those early, messy drafts. Seth Godin, your creativity and friendship put wind beneath my wings that carried me across the world and back. Thank you.

My sister Beth supported my spirit throughout, just as she did with *The Blue Sweater*. Beth, I love our collaborations, and your generosity astonishes.

Carlyle Singer, Acumen's fearless president, is my partner in building both an institution and a movement. She made it possible for me to write this book while remaining close to the work. Thank you, Carlyle, for modeling shared leadership and for being a friend.

I could not have completed the book without the big-hearted support of a small and mighty group at Acumen who helped do whatever it took to organize and reconsider fragments and journals of stories told and untold: Lindsay Camacho, Charlotte Erb, Sonya Khattak, and Maureen Klein. Lynn Roland helped make this our shared book. Thank you to patient readers who gave truthful, constructive feedback: Sophia Ahmed, Wei Wei Hsing, Esha Mufti, Chee Pearlman, and, of course, my mother, the most voracious reader I know. Thanks to Regional Directors for your patience through this process, for your ideas, for teaching me more than you know. Thanks to Sunny Bates, Karie Brown, Leslie Gimbel, Jeanie Honey, Otho Kerr, and Taylor Milsal for your endless support.

I feel like the luckiest woman on earth to do work I adore with people I love. Thanks to the entire Acumen team across the globe. You model the principles of this book, teach me daily, and inspire me to be a better version of myself. Your commitment to excellence has helped build four new organizations in our extended family—Acumen's off-grid energy fund KawiSafi, our agriculture resiliency fund ARAF, our Latin America Growth Fund, and our spin-off from Lean Data, 60 Decibels. Each of those teams, too, have influenced the ideas in this book, and for all of you, I am grateful.

I interviewed many Acumen entrepreneurs and fellows

both on-site and at distance and appreciate every visit, every interaction. Each one of you has taught me more than I can say. And though many of your stories and lessons about making capital work for us are not included here, nothing is wasted. Indeed, the collection of Acumen's nearly 130 entrepreneurs and 600 fellows around the world represents a treasure trove of human possibility; all of you have lessons worth sharing.

Many thanks go to Acumen's phenomenal board of directors who encouraged me to write this book in the first place: our indominable chair Shaiza Rizavi, Andrea Soros Colombel, Cristina Ljungberg, Hunter Boll, Julius Gaudio, Kathleen Chew Wai Lin, Kirsten Nevill-Manning, Margo Alexander, Nate Laurell, Pat Mitchell, Stuart Davidson, Thulasiraj Ravilla, as well as Dave Heller, William Mayer, Robert Niehaus, Mike Novogratz, and Ali Siddiqui, who only recently rolled off the board after many years of service. Thank you to every advisory member (I'm including those not acknowledged elsewhere): Jawad Aslam, Diana Barrett, Tim Brown, Peter Cain, Niko Canner, Jesse Clarke, Beth Comstock, Rebecca Eastmond, Paul Fletcher, Katherine Fulton, Peter Goldmark, Per Heggenes, Katie Hill, Arianna Huffington, Jill Iscol, Maria Angeles Leon Lopez, Federica Marchionni, Felipe Medina, Susan Meiselas, Craig Nevill-Manning, Noor Pahlavi, Paul Polman, Kerry J. Sulkowicz, Vikki Tam, Mark Tercek, Pat Tierney, Daniel Toole, and Hamdi Ulukaya. For your constant support, thank you. And, of course, none of this learning would have been possible without Acumen's remarkable community of partners, course takers, supporters, and friends around the world. When all is said and done, you are the vanguard.

These pages carry the written wisdom of individuals far wiser than I will ever be. I cannot possibly name all of them, but the writings of Chinua Achebe, David Brooks, John Gardner,

Anand Giridharadas, Seth Godin, Jon Haidt, Marie Howe, Chris Lowney, Maria Popova, Bryan Stevenson, Pádraig Ó Tuama, Elaine Pagels, Amartya Sen, and Krista Tippett especially have been a gift. I also owe much to the Good Society Readings and friends from the Aspen Institute, where I am a trustee and proud Henry Crown fellow.

Thank you to the Rockefeller Foundation who supported me with a monthlong residency at its Bellagio Conference Center. That time helped me get started and introduced me to a community of encouraging friends. Thanks to Akhil Gupta as well.

Belonging to a big, crazy, loving family not only grounds me but makes my life richer and my work more effective and expansive. I'm forever grateful to my parents, Barbara and Bob; to my siblings, Robert, Michael, Elizabeth, John, Amy, and Matthew; my in-laws, Sukey, Cortney, Tina, Nadean, and Mike. To my stepdaughters Elizabeth and Anna and their spouses, Joseph and Sam. And to the next big generation of family members who will change the world along with their peers. It is for you and every other young person on this planet that I ultimately wrote this book.

Finally, to my darling Chris, for your patient ear, your constant support, for your forever love, for everything.

ABOUT THE AUTHOR

Jacqueline Novogratz is the *New York Times* bestselling author of *The Blue Sweater*. In 2001, she founded Acumen with the idea of investing philanthropic "patient capital" in entrepreneurs seeking to solve the toughest issues of poverty. A pioneer of "impact investing," Acumen and its investments have brought critical services like health care, education, and clean energy to hundreds of millions of low-income people. After supporting hundreds of social entrepreneurs, Jacqueline and her team recognized character as the primary driver of success; in 2020 they launched Acumen Academy as the world's school for social change. Under Jacqueline's leadership, Acumen also has launched several for-profit impact funds designed to invest at the intersection of poverty and climate change and has spun off 60 Decibels, a company that measures social impact, founded on the principle that serving stakeholders is as important as enriching shareholders.

Jacqueline has been named one of the Top 100 Global Thinkers by *Foreign Policy* and one of the world's 100 Greatest Living Business Minds by *Forbes*, which also honored her with the Forbes 400 Lifetime Achievement Award for Social Entrepreneurship. In addition to her work with Acumen, she is a sought-after speaker and sits on a number of philanthropic boards. She lives in New York City with her husband.